# Lemons and Lace

## *From* Bitterness to Beauty

*A Journey through
the Death of a Child,
Cancer, Betrayal and the
Suicide of a Husband*

# PAM FLEMING

www.wavedancermedia.com

Text and cover design by: Karen Webb

ISBN: 978-1523715329

For Worldwide Distribution, Printed in the U.S.A.

# Dedication

I want to dedicate this book to my wonderful husband Dave Fleming, who has been so supportive and encouraging during this process. He has been a great sounding board and very truthful especially when I used the same word too many times. (I'm smiling.)

Again to my daughter Megan Mosemann, who bravely held my hand during my time of grief even though she was experiencing a tremendous loss in her own life. She is truly an example of Christ's love.

To my son Nathan Nicely of whom I am extremely proud. Thank you for your courage in serving our country for over 20 years and also being a man of honor.

To my mom, Deborah Botteicher who fervently prayed for me and loved me in my darkest hours.

And most to my Savior and Lord Jesus Christ, for bringing about healing and restoration in my times of despair, and giving me strength to hold on to my life and my faith.

# Acknowledgements

I'm so thankful for the help of Dave Peterson, my publisher and coach from Wave Dancer Media. He stretched me and for that I am very grateful. He had faith in a "Rookie" writer and always told me I could do it, even when I thought it wasn't possible. Thank you for your heartfelt prayers Dave, and for the times you urged me to dig deeper.

I would like to thank Pastor Dave Hess, for being obedient to the Lord, and speaking a profound *word* into my heart during my greatest need. The *word*, "Your life will not end in tragedy" was a healing balm that began my process of wholeness.

To Karen Webb who brought so much joy into this process, not to mention her unbelievable talent.

Thank you Karen for the beautiful cover you've designed, and the layout of the text.

To Dominique Abney—a multitalented woman of God who edited my manuscript, created a fantastic website and gave great advice for using other social media outlets.

Three special ladies I would like to acknowledge are, Pat Dupert who sat with me in my darkest hour and helped bring healing into my heart through her gifted ministry. Maryann Hartman, who helped me edit, before it got to the editor and offered many suggestions and helpful hints. I am grateful for our new found friendship. And to Zoe Monserrate, who has the beautiful gift of encouragement and has been an amazing prayer warrior and friend.

Thanks to my Prayer Team, I always knew you were covering me in thoughtful, loving prayers:

Deborah Botteicher (My mom)

Megan Mosemann (My daughter)

Sheila Maier

Betty Shanyfelt

Cindy Martin

Cynthia Bevin

Julie Hall

Lynda Thrush

Mary Loe

Pat Dupert

Sandra Kuehn

Shawntel Morton

Sheri Hess

Zoe Monserrate

Eileen Gallagher

# Endorsements

I highly recommend Pam Fleming's new book to you. Pam's authentic, raw, painful life story includes her husband's suicide, the loss of her daughter, her battle with cancer, and betrayal...while eventually finding hope and grace from her God in the midst of extremely stressful circumstances. This book does not offer pat answers, but it offers great hope. Thank you, Pam, for your honesty and openness to share personal experiences that few people seem to be willing to talk about. This book will help many facing tragic life experiences that have no easy answers. This book is a treasure.

Larry Kreider
International Director
DOVE International
Author of more than 35 books

We live in a world where people rarely make eye contact. Perhaps we feel if we really let another person look into our eyes, they will see our imperfections. The stories of our struggles can be difficult for us to own or even bring to the forefront of our conscious thoughts. We work tirelessly to make sure everything looks "just right" on the outside. The stakes are high when it comes to telling the truth about who we are and where we've been. It's often easier to keep quiet—and look away.

The book you hold in your hands was penned by a courageous woman who stepped out of the security of remaining hidden to look you straight in the eye and tell you her unedited story. Her story—filled with unspeakable pain—will give you the will to engage with your own struggles and move through them to whole-heartedly engage with life.

Impossible?

You may feel that way right now. But as you join Pam in her walk of faith—you will discover a path from your darkness into the light. Walking into the light by facing our story is hard, but not nearly as difficult as spending our lives running from it. Embracing our imperfection is risky, but not nearly as devastating as giving up on love, joy and belonging. Only when we are brave enough to explore the darkness will we discover the amazing power of the light.

Thank you, Pam, for showing us the way to move forward—courageously plunging into compassion and connection with the people we love and the life we were meant to live!

Sheri Hess
Co-author of *Beautiful One*

Tragedy triumphs over faith for many who have gone through life crises on the level that this author has. How can you experience caring for a sickly child then losing them, add to that the betrayal of the two most important people in your life, the suicide of a husband, all while you're standing on the promises of a loving Father? In her well titled book "Lemons and Lace" Pam takes us with her on her life's journey of being able to live again through adversities that most people would never ever want to experience.

Her ability to trust again despite her life tragedies will inspire the weakest person in their faith to live an overcoming life. I found this book so inspiring and filled with hope for the desperate seeker of a purpose filled life. Thank you Pam!

Trisha Frost
Co-author of:
*Unbound: Breaking Free of Life's Entanglements*
and *Spiritual Slavery to Spiritual Sonship*

# Table of Contents

# Foreword

Jesus said, *"In the world you will have tribulation."* John 16:33 (NKJV) "Tribulation." It's a strong word. It refers to more than flat tires and stuck traffic. It describes moments so difficult, they threaten to crush your very soul.

Pam has had her share of such moments. Disease, disappointment, betrayal and traumas so intense— they did threaten to crush her soul.

Yet, in the middle of it all, she found the next part of Jesus' statement to be equally true: *"...but be of good cheer, for I have overcome the world."* John 16:33 (NKJV) She discovered His healing hope in the times of crushing storms.

She didn't attain peace through sheer determination. She found there is no easy formula for these kinds of things.

Instead, she was drawn closer to a very real Shepherd who fully understands the dark valleys we walk through. He walked through His own tribulations. And He walks with us through ours, too.

As you read Pam's story, I invite you to join her in marveling at the faithfulness of God. I invite you to see life through her eyes, gazing into the eyes of Jesus—the man of sorrows. One who is well-acquainted with the things that grieve us. I also invite you to let Him gaze into your soul—loving you, healing you, and drawing your heart ever closer to His.

Dave Hess
Senior Pastor
Christ Community Church
Camp Hill, Pennsylvania

# Introduction

The kind man at the funeral home handed me a white bag. This seemed routine for him but for me it was quite surreal—like walking through a fog, a senseless, numbing fog.

"Mrs. Nicely, if there's anything you need, don't hesitate to call," he said. Later in the car, I would burst into tears. My stomach so twisted I wanted to be sick. He didn't know that in just a few short days I would be calling him—asking if I could return the bag and its contents. Thinking back, I'm sure it was probably one of the most bizarre questions he'd ever heard.

I was so desperate to have my husband back that I couldn't think straight. Distraught with the thought of never seeing Rick as he was—a beautiful, talented, loving husband—made my whole body shake. Yes, I knew I would see him in heaven, but for now all that remained was in *that bag*.

Just like all the other times I'd used my husband's car, I opened the trunk, my son placed the bag inside, and we drove away. Fortunately, my son Nathan and his wife Kate were with me at that time. They were heading home after spending three weeks caring for and helping me deal with my new life as a grieving widow. A grieving widow...it was inconceivable.

The reality of everything I was and had been for the last thirty-four years was in *that bag:* the dutiful, ever-smiling, "move on to the next thing" pastor's wife; the televangelists' wife. That bag...I felt *that bag* was all that was left of my life. We were successful as other folks saw it. We lived well, shared the Lord with many, and followed the Bible. But, I would learn—and am still learning—that even when you follow the Word of God as if it were a recipe, your life doesn't always turn out like the picture in the cookbook. All of my memories, my hopes and dreams for my twilight years, were there in *that bag*—in the trunk of my husband's car.

# 1

## House of Mercy

Rick and I met at Bob Jones University as adults. Earlier in our lives, as children, we had met at a church summer camp. Rick was a tall, handsome man with coal-black hair and a beautiful smile. He Loved God and had a true calling on his life. Even as a young man, you could see his dedication and fire to serve the Lord. Besides his great charm, he was smart and knew what he wanted to do in his life—

**Our wedding day.**

and that was to be a Pastor. I approached him while at Bob Jones University and reminded him of our childhood meeting. As I walked away, he later told me that he said to himself, "I'm going to marry her," and that he did!

## COMING TO FAITH

We were married eight months later and honeymooned for a week in Niagara Falls. Our first call was to serve at a little country church, him as the pastor and I as the faithful pastor's wife. We were filled with the anticipation of how God was going to use us.

Rick was called to be a pastor at the age of nine while sitting on a rock, out in the woods at a church camp. He knew at that moment God was calling him and he devoted his life to serve the Lord. I came to know the Lord at age thirteen, after reading a book titled *The Human Garbage Can*. It was about how our mouths are like a garbage can and how Jesus can renew us. It spoke to me, and I asked the Lord to forgive me. It's funny how many times before that, I remember going to different kids' clubs and hearing the Gospel, but it never really sunk in. God had planted a seed in me—one that would soon burst forth in faith.

When I was young, we had a gentleman named Mr. Wilt who lived across the street from my childhood home. He was a very loving, Christian man and my mom told me how he was always trying to preach to her and get her to go to church with him and his wife. God was certainly pursuing her. She also had a boss who relentlessly witnessed to her; and at the age of thirty-five, she gave her life over to Christ. I came to the Lord a few months later. From that time on, it was both our desire to serve the Lord and tell everyone we knew what happened to us.

We had a swimming pool in our back yard and I would invite our friends over to swim. We invariably ended up talking about the Lord and how He changed us. Several of my best friends got saved around that pool. That pool was a symbol of how water purifies—cleans our souls. It was like the Pool of Bethesda found in John 5:4 (NKJV):

> *"For an angel went down at a certain time into the pool and stirred up the water; then whoever stepped in first, after the stirring of the water, was made well of whatever disease he had."*

Bethesda means "House of Mercy." We had wonderful summers, seeing kids come to know Jesus at our house of mercy.

As I grew in the Lord I thought for sure, when I became older, I would be a missionary in some remote part of Africa. I was relieved when God called me to serve as a pastor's wife in the states. Little did I know how difficult, painful, and heart wrenching it would be to fulfill this mission. Being a pastor or a pastor's wife for twenty-five years is certainly not for the faint in heart.

## FIRST CHURCHES

We first served at a small community church near Ligonier, Pennsylvania. Here, there were many firsts—our first calling, our first family of believers, and our first baby. God blessed us with a little boy. He was a big blue eyed son with curly blonde locks and a pleasing personality. We called him Nathan which means "to give." He was an easy child and brought a lot of laughter and joy into our lives.

Traveling to Ligonier took us thirty minutes every Sunday morning, Sunday night, and Wednesday night. We didn't mind the drive; we loved what we were doing and felt like we were in the right place. However, there were times we got stuck in the mountains of Ligonier in huge snowstorms. After hours of traveling through treacherous highways, we would make it home and say to ourselves, "Do we really want to do this?" Of course the answer was always "Yes!" The people at that little country church were gracious and sweet to us. Yet, as in any church, there are always obstacles to overcome. We were young and had a lot to learn about ministry and people in general.

I remember one of our first invites to dinner. The woman invited us over for stuffed pork chops and told us to come straight from church. We were excited because we were finally building community. As it turned out, when we got there, the pork chops weren't even out of the freezer yet. While she was preparing the meal, I ended up doing what seemed like a week's worth of dishes. Afterwards, we were so glad to get on the road and go home. We definitely had a few laughs over that, and as a young wife I learned to always get the pork chops out of the freezer before the guests arrive.

After a year of serving part time, we asked the elders if they would be willing to take us on full-time if we would relocate closer to the church. They had no interest in that, so we felt called to move on. We said goodbye to our first little church and started pastoring at a Baptist church. This was very exciting because the church provided a parsonage next door. They offered Rick a full time position, although throughout our ministry he always had to take on another job to sustain us.

At the Baptist church, the family of believers were so loving and caring. Every Sunday, it would only be seconds before someone would snatch Nathan up. Everyone loved him and wanted to play with him, or hold him. It was wonderful to see the outpouring of love towards our son. Life seemed pretty perfect at that time. A great church, a nice family...things were good. We served the Lord with vigor, hoping to change the world as most young people do. My husband was a very passionate pastor and did a great job of caring for the sheep. Although we made many mistakes—had been hurt and hurt others—we had a true desire to do God's work.

I soon became pregnant with our second child. As we waited for the baby's arrival, I felt uneasy about the pregnancy, but my doctor assured me everything was absolutely fine. Our little girl arrived two weeks late. We picked out the name Elizabeth which means "the promise of God."

## THE BIRTH OF ELIZABETH

I remember the day Elizabeth was born. It was June 15, 1977 at a hospital in Greensburg, Pennsylvania. Since she was two weeks late it was such a relief to finally know she was coming. After only an hour of hard labor, I was taken to the delivery room. In those days you didn't get ultrasounds to see if you were having a boy or girl, so it was always a surprise. We were hoping for a girl because we already had our boy Nathan.

Moments after she was born, I recall my husband falling on the floor in the delivery room. He passed out cold from the look he saw on the doctor's face. When the doctor saw her little deformed ear, he knew there was an issue and immediately told us there was a problem. How do you react to such a thing? Do you scream? Do you deny? Or, do you just cry? I don't remember my immediate reaction other than feeling fear, fear that our little girl was going to die.

Elizabeth was born with a single lung, one kidney, and a deformed right ear. "I'm sorry Mr. and Mrs. Nicely, but your little girl will probably not make it through the night. She is struggling hard to breathe and has other critical issues."

The next thing we knew, she was being rushed to Children's Hospital in Pittsburgh which was forty-five minutes to an hour away. My husband and my mom left immediately, leaving me at the hospital wondering what was happening. It was devastating not being able to be there with my husband and mother. The hospital where I delivered Elizabeth wasn't getting any information. I didn't know why they weren't updating me on how my child was doing. Was it wrong for me to expect such a thing? It seemed as though the nurses were afraid to come into my room. Perhaps they thought they would say something that would upset me.

It was few and far between that anyone visited me during my stay. My expectations were that the hospital would take care of me, maybe send a pastor or someone to comfort and take care of my spiritual and/or emotional needs. I had to make a request for things that normally should have been done. No one from the church came to see me. Like the nurses, they may have felt uncomfortable with the situation—not knowing what to say. Maybe they didn't know how I would react. All I knew was that I needed someone who was strong to pray for me and be with me—a friend...anyone.

I realized it was hard for people to face me, but I knew they were praying. Still, my heart was broken when not one person visited. This situation taught me an extremely valuable lesson about the importance of being there for others, no matter what the circumstance. It's a lesson I've never forgotten. After two more agonizing days in the hospital, I was finally discharged and able to travel to Pittsburgh to see our little girl.

It's a dreadful feeling to leave the hospital, after giving birth, without a baby in your arms. I'm sure other women who have experienced a miscarriage, death, or critical illness of a child have felt the same emptiness and distress. To this day my heart goes out to moms who have lost their babies—knowing firsthand the agony that they've experienced.

## EXPECTATIONS
## AND DISAPPOINTMENT

Preparing for a new life to enter your household is usually accompanied by setting up a nursery. Also, followed by friends giving amazing baby showers with everything you need to care for a new, sweet member of your family. I was no different. My nursery was decorated in neutral tones for either a boy or girl, and it was darling. I was showered with plenty of new sleepers, diapers, and all the things you love to look at before the arrival of your newborn. There is nothing more exciting than going into your new baby's nursery before they are born and checking out all the new fun stuff—arranging it, refolding it, even just holding it. Imagining what your child will look like is exciting. "Will they look like me or my husband, maybe even Mimi or Pap?" Secretly, in your heart, you're hoping that maybe they'll be the spitting image of you. A girl can always dream.

When you're pregnant with a child your expectations are great, so real, and full of promise. The bond between a mother and child is something that cannot be explained or appreciated by anyone other than a mother. When those expectations are not met, and the stark reality sets in, there is disappointment—a disappointment that cannot be quenched, except by the grace of God.

My disappointment was immense. My little girl, who I had longed for, would possibly not even survive. The reality was that I didn't give birth to a perfect child. Elizabeth had serious medical conditions and needed constant care. I wasn't prepared for such a journey. After the initial shock was over and the realization set in, I was able to mentally deal with the fact that I had the responsibility of a sick child to care for. God's mercy and His grace needed to be my constant lifeline.

> *But he said to me, "My grace is sufficient for you, for my power is made perfect in weakness." Therefore I will boast all the more gladly about my weaknesses, so that Christ's power may rest on me.* 2 Corinthians 12:9 (NIV)

# 2

# Elizabeth

For the following month, I traveled back and forth, from the hospital, learning how to care for our very sick child. Elizabeth's trachea was bent so she was unable to drink liquids without choking. The nurses had to teach me the technique to allow her to drink, and all the other things I needed to know for her daily care. It was a long grueling month, but I was happy to be at the hospital and see our baby girl. I chose not to spend the nights there because I had our two-year-old son, Nathan, to care for as well. I couldn't be totally missing from his life for such a long time.

After a month, they sent her home and told us to take care of her as best we could. The day she came home was so exciting and we were full of hope; although, we were told that her chances of survival were slim. Armed with a suction machine and an oxygen tent—to help with her breathing—we took her home believing God was going to do a miraculous healing. It was a very scary undertaking. I was in no way a nurse and yet I had to make sure her oxygen tent was operating and that I could properly use it. The suction machine was a strange looking apparatus that sounded like a jackhammer.

The thoughts of her not eating were continually on my mind. I was also concerned that she would have trouble breathing while eating. I was fearful I would not be able to care for her the way I should. It seemed like an awesome responsibility for a layperson, but God truly gave us grace and the ability to care for her needs. Our faith was strong and we were confident that God would heal our little girl.

## CARING FOR A SICK CHILD

Having a sick child is not an easy task. Our first child was so healthy. Although you go through a lot of adjustments with a new healthy little person in your home, you can't prepare yourself for what it takes to care for an ailing child. We had many sleepless nights, harrowing days, and several stays at the hospital.

Every night she would wake when we got up to refill the ice in the oxygen tank. Then we had to suction her out in order for her to eat. There were no microwaves back then so preparing her baby oatmeal was done the old fashioned way. I was so grateful for a fabulous invention called an Infa-Feeder. It allowed her to eat some solid food.

Many times after suctioning, although she cried from hunger, she would be too exhausted to eat. We were frustrated and sad. We would cry out for God to heal her and as the months past, we prayed "God, please heal Elizabeth or take her home to be with You." Our anguish was great because we were always concerned for her life.

**Elizabeth**

It's hard on your nerves and saddens your heart to think that your own flesh and blood could be taken from you at any time. We took her to a couple of faith healers and had many people praying for her. We loved her and cared for her, always believing for a miraculous healing.

People in our area knew about Elizabeth and our situation because a local newspaper did an article on her, helping us to raise funds to help us financially. The oxygen tank alone was one-hundred dollars a day; and on our salary, it was an absolute fortune. Many donated to our cause and we believed that all of our needs would be met; and they were. It was

amazing how generous and loving people can be—
strangers that don't know you, but are touched by a
sick child.

I recall how difficult it was to function, taking
care of Nathan, caring for Elizabeth, and trying
to hold on to our faith. Each evening, Rick and
I would pray for our little girl. "God please heal
Elizabeth." When we closed our eyes to sleep, the
enemy would attempt to put terrible thoughts in
our heads—thoughts that she wouldn't make it
through the night. It was a time in our life that we
relied heavily on God's grace and mercy.

Being up several times at night, trying to care
for our child, was difficult. However, God gave us
strength in our weariness. It was a hard and exhausting
time. So hard that at times we thought we wouldn't
make it through another day. We were grouchy and
tired, but realized we had many responsibilities. We
had a congregation that counted on us, jobs to do, a
house to clean, cooking—all the everyday things still
needed to be done.

## HELPERS, REBUKE, AND
## MORE STRETCHING

Finding people to watch Elizabeth when we
needed to be away for a few hours was difficult. They
were afraid that something would happen while we

were gone and didn't want that kind of responsibility. We certainly understood that, but there was one woman—my best friend at the time—who would babysit for us on occasion. Her name was Emma. She was about fifty years older than me, and we had a beautiful connection.

Emma raised ten children of her own and nothing scared her. She adored Elizabeth and was loving and kind to our baby girl. She would come over to the house so that we could do grocery shopping or any other errand that needed done. Sometimes it was just for us to spend quality time with our son Nathan. She would sit and rock

**Elizabeth sleeping.**

Elizabeth, sing to her, and just love on her. I have many fond memories of Emma and will never forget her. She was no doubt sent by God and showed the genuine love of Christ to us and our baby.

One day, one of our elders came to us and told us the reason Elizabeth was born deformed was probably because of sin in our life. The hurt of what he said made me very angry; I remember having a few choice words with this "gentleman." Rick, not saying a word, sat quietly as I expressed my feelings. How could this man not realize how crushing it would be to make such an inappropriate statement? I suppose our self-righteousness gets in the way of our reasoning at times. We should think about and be more aware of our misconceptions of others, especially when they are going through difficult times. Nonetheless, the elder's statement caused us to examine our lives. We wondered, "Could this be true? Were we wretched sinners thinking our hearts were pure?" We were very young and grew up in a church atmosphere that was judgmental. We knew in our hearts that this wasn't true and just wanted to do what God called us to do. Did his statement make us angry? Of course we had anger. Did we feel hurt? Yes, very hurt. We moved on and nothing more was said about the incident.

My mom came to help out by caring for Elizabeth during the day and was there for support. One night we heard a terrible scream from mom. We jumped out of bed thinking that maybe Elizabeth had died in the middle of the night—although, we couldn't imagine my mom reacting in this way. Later, we found that she had gotten up to use the bathroom, and not wanting to wake Elizabeth, hadn't turned on any lights. She went to the wrong doorway and fell down a flight of steps breaking her back in a few places. It was devastating. You feel as though you're being stretched to the very limit of who you are mentally, physically and spiritually.

## THE ALTAR OF SACRIFICE

A few days after the incident with my mother, Rick and I were feeling overwhelmed. We went to the churchyard one night in tears pleading to God to heal Elizabeth or take her home. It had been fourteen months and we were growing weary. We loved her. She was our little fighter, our child with spunk. Then God spoke to us, "Are you willing for me not to heal her or take her home? Are you willing to take care of her with all of her disabilities?"

That's not what we wanted. It seemed so hard, so tiring. After a time of great mourning, we both agreed that if it was God's will, we would be willing to do it. We felt like Abraham who had taken his son to the mountain to sacrifice him to God. I know Rick's heart was breaking, as was mine. We held each other and cried until we couldn't cry anymore. We had finally given our baby over to God and accepted whatever His plans were for her. We learned that day that our life was not our own. He asked us to place her life and ours on the altar of sacrifice, which was hard to do.

"Why would God do such a thing?" is a question many have asked in similar circumstances. I believe that our children are gifts that God gives us to care for. They are His children before they are ours. They belong to Him and we are blessed when He entrusts us with these little lives…no matter what the circumstance.

## A QUIET PASSING

Two weeks later on a hot summer day in August, Elizabeth was extremely lethargic, awake, but very listless. I decided to take her over to my chiropractor. She didn't like her visits, but I felt it gave her some relief. I had taken her many times before, so I thought it would be helpful. He adjusted her as he usually did but she didn't respond. Usually she screamed, but this day she remained completely calm.

I took her home and she slept. I kept waking her and tried to feed her. I bathed her, but she was still not responding. This went on all day; she just wasn't herself. I put her back to bed that night. Rick and I were very anxious so we decided to wallpaper our bedroom. All that nervous energy needed to be put to good use. I checked on her about every half hour and at 2:00 am, I went into her room and she was gone.

What's it like seeing your child lay there, still, and unresponsive? It takes your breath away—even if a part of you knew it was inevitable.

At that moment, our souls were filled not only with waves of grief, but guilt, anger, and disbelief. It's hard to believe the guilt that comes upon you when you have a sick child…you feel as though you could have done something to save them. You ask yourself, "What if I had done this or that?" Anger is only present because your greatest desire is to have God heal this precious little person. This child who should have been born perfect and at her age of fourteen months—walking, laughing, and starting to talk—was laying still without breath. Disbelief comes because no more than an hour ago, she was sleeping in her bed and now she is dead. Your only comfort comes in knowing that she is with her Creator and is completely whole and happy.

## THE TRIP TO THE HOSPITAL

We were left grieving and wondering what she would have been, who would she have married, how many grandchildren would she have given us, and what special gift did God give her to serve Him? Of course we called the hospital, and they told us that a coroner could not come unless her doctor had pronounced her dead, but her doctor was out of town. Unfortunately, 911 was not available at that time so we didn't know what else to do. The voice on the other end of the line told us to take her to the emergency room. It was the middle of the night. We called a friend to come and watch Nathan so we could take our beautiful daughter to the hospital to be pronounced dead.

The trip to the hospital wasn't long, but it seemed like an eternity. I wrapped Elizabeth in her baby blanket and held on to her tight. Rick drove the car in silence, tears streaming down his face. His strength was evident to me; he was a wonderful father to both of our children and an extremely compassionate man. He stayed strong for me throughout this whole journey, even though his pain was just as great as mine. This would be the last time that I got to be a mom and he got to be a dad to our precious little girl.

To know that the next time we would see her, she would be with Jesus, fully alive and healed, running to us with open arms, gave us *hope beyond reason*.[1]

Holding my dead child in my arms was so surreal and yet the grace of God was so strong. I had a peace that was indescribable. How could this be? Only God can give such a peace. How do people survive without God in their lives? It's truly unthinkable and hard for me to imagine.

We arrived at the hospital and everyone's concern for Rick and I was apparent. The medical staff offered us tranquilizers to ease the pain and shock. We were quite numb and disoriented already, so we refused. Taking medication can mask the pain and may make you unable to deal with your grief, although, sometimes it's necessary. I had lost a piece of myself, a part of my heart that day. I felt that no drug could remedy that loss or take away the pain. We were feeling as Rachel did in Matthew 2:18. Rachel died while giving birth to Benjamin, but it was prophesied that Rachel was weeping for an entire nation during the birth. It's a mourning that tears your gut out. The only genuine comfort we can receive is in the arms of Jesus.

*"A voice was heard in Ramah, weeping and loud wailing, Rachel weeping for her children, and she did not want to be comforted, because they were gone."* Matthew 2:18 (NET)

## TRUSTING

To this day I am grateful. It's truly a miracle I didn't put my faith in drugs or dig myself into a deep dark hole from which I could never get out. This is the kind of faith that only God can give as we continue to put our trust in Him. The kind of faith that even in the darkest part of your life, when you feel stripped of everything, hope is still possible. When we think there is no way out, we come to find there truly is a way to overcome. Even if you feel as though you want to curl up in a ball and live your life on the couch, I want you to know that you can survive and come out on top. Psalm 30:11-12 (NKJV) says:

*"You have turned for me my mourning into dancing; You have put off my sackcloth and clothed me with gladness, to the end that my glory may sing praise to You and not be silent. O LORD my God, I will give thanks to You forever."*

I know some may wonder what I'm talking about. "How can you possibly give glory to God for such an event in your life? He took your child!" I certainly don't want to seem self-righteous and have you think that I didn't have anger, because I did. Sometimes I thought I wouldn't make it. I even wanted to die. This is grief; and at some point in your life, you will probably have to experience it. Let God do the healing in whatever way He sees fit. I know it isn't easy. You can't wave a magic wand and have your grief be gone, but God can help. You just have to trust Him.

There is still a part of my heart missing. When you lose a child, the pain goes away, but you still grieve that missing part of your heart. I don't remember Rick's feelings at that time, other than tears and sadness. He lost his little girl too.

## A MISTAKE

A week after we buried Elizabeth, the memorial park called and told us that they made a mistake and put her in the wrong burial plot. They informed us that we would need to be at the cemetery when they removed the casket and put her in the correct plot. Rick went, I just couldn't. The thought of seeing that tiny white casket was unbearable, something I just couldn't do.

*"How is it even possible that this could have occurred? God, haven't we been through enough?"* were questions I screamed to God. It was like putting salt on an open wound. My heart of compassion made me think of how the funeral director must have felt when he made the call to us. I'm sure his anguish was real and his heart was broken to be the bearer of such terrible news.

## GUILT

The following year was difficult. When a child dies—as I mentioned earlier—no matter how they pass you live with some guilt. The wondering questions of "Could we have done more? Was it our fault?" plagued our minds. We knew these were lies from the enemy, but we both still battled with these thoughts. We missed her terribly, and our son, only two years old at the time of Elizabeth's death, missed her too. One day he had a sister he called Bisbeth, and the next day she was gone. We didn't realize that a child that young could feel some of the pain we felt. This became most apparent when he entered her room each morning and asked, "Where's Bisbeth?" with concern on his face.

Explaining to him that his little sister went to live with Jesus was challenging to say the least. You could see that he missed her. He just wanted to see his baby sister again. I will never know the extent of grief that Nathan went through. We needed to give so much care and time to Elizabeth. Sometimes I sensed his sadness as we would drop him off at a babysitter's house or when we would spend endless hours caring for his sister. To this day, I'm not sure how it may have affected his life. Part of me believes that God takes care of the hearts of little children, so I trust Him concerning the effects it has had on our son.

Losing a child is very hard on a marriage, but we later weathered that storm. Statistics show that a high percentage of marriages do not survive the death of a child. Working on mending your own heart from guilt, blame, and sadness is an extremely painful process. The thought of caring for your spouse's grief, as well, is far too challenging. Having been through it, I can see how all these things can cause the deterioration of a relationship.

## MARRIAGE AND ENDURANCE

Our strong faith in the Lord was a huge factor in the endurance of our marriage. It may well have been the only thing keeping us going. We always believed in Mark 10:9 (NASB):

*"What therefore God has joined together, let no man separate."*

Our love was strong. We made a decision to hold onto one another and to let God do the healing in our hearts. We knew He could strengthen our marriage in spite of, and through the devastation.

When I say we made a decision, I mean it literally. We didn't wake up one morning and say, "Oh let's stay together because we love each other and God said it's the right thing to do." No, it's a true decision that can only be made because of our relationship with our Lord.

It doesn't matter how your child dies, or what tragedy you experience, the element of guilt usually appears. It is a strange phenomenon when you think of it, and it can bring strange thoughts— like one partner secretly blaming another or just feeling like "What's the use of staying married?"

Rick and I made a covenant with each other on our wedding day, October 5, 1974. Our decision was based on that covenant—no matter our feelings or how hurt we were about the death of our child. I believe when people have unfounded anger towards God, it seems to show itself in the relationship with the person they are closest to. Usually it's our spouse. In God's hands, we survived that difficult situation.

## A TESTIMONY

Many people knew of Elizabeth and were praying for her. We learned after her death that a young man in Florida was touched by her story and had come to know the Lord. Even our tiny little angel had a part in someone coming into the Kingdom. We will never know the full reason for her short life until we are with the Lord. I am grateful and honored that God gave us the opportunity to be a part of her life. Psalm 127:3 (NIV) says:

*"Children are a heritage from the LORD, offspring a reward from him."*

## A NEW LIFE

After losing a child, you long to hold them in your arms and feel them close to you again. I remember the yearning I had to care for and cuddle a baby. We both knew that we wanted more children, but felt apprehensive after what we had gone through with Elizabeth.

God knew the cry of our hearts and a few months later I was pregnant. We were excited and nervous at the same time. No one could replace our darling little daughter, but we dreamed about having another little girl.

I remember my mom telling me that she felt it would be a girl with curly hair and blue eyes. We were hopeful, but of course if it was a boy, we would be just as happy. Nine months later, after only one hour of labor, I delivered a lovely baby girl. We named her Megan, which means "Pearl" and she certainly was and still is today. Now a godly woman with six children of her own, she has beautiful long curly hair and bright blue eyes. I am grateful not only that she is my child, but she has been my rock and a true friend.

## Endnote

1. Hess, Dave. *Hope Beyond Reason.* Createspace Independent Publishing Platform, 2014.
   An uplifting, true story of our pastor's journey through cancer and God's miraculous healing. A story of hope for anyone walking through dark times.

# 3

## The "C" Word

It was 1982 and we felt our time in the Baptist church was over. We moved to my hometown in Altoona, Pennsylvania and worked alongside my mother and another pastor for a time. With guidance from God, we went out on our own and founded the Altoona Full Gospel Church in 1984.

Our first meeting was at the local YWCA. It was a beautiful spring morning in May. There was no air conditioning in the building and it was quite stuffy so we opened the door. There were about thirty people in attendance with a lot of excitement and anticipation in the air.

When my husband got up to preach, a bumble bee came in and was buzzing around everyone; a distraction for sure. People were ducking and flinching until Rick finally pointed at the bee and said, "Be gone in the name of Jesus!" The bee went straight out the door. We all laughed. It made a memorable story for our first service together.

We put our heart and souls into every aspect of the church. I worked with the worship team, all the social events, prayer and women's ministry. Rick was the lead pastor and was a very dedicated man. Even then I knew that he carried a heavy load and felt the pressure of founding a new church. I think many pastors feel that way when trying to get a new ministry off the ground.

## THE FIRST SIGN

The church was doing great and although not large in size, we had a wonderful group of about a one-hundred dedicated people. We were having fun and enjoying the experience. In 1986, a group of women and I were in intercessory prayer. I had been coughing for a few months and was thinking I may have had allergies or a long lingering cold. One day in prayer one of the ladies gave a word that she saw a black spot on my lung. The group immediately prayed for healing and I had no doubt that God would do a work and heal the problem.

After months of continued coughing and dry heaves, I decided it was time to see a doctor. I had been foolish to ignore my symptoms. My faith in my healing kept me believing I would be well. It was the era of the charismatic movement, so for me to doubt was not acceptable. It's funny how our common sense is sometimes overridden when we believe very strongly in the healing power of God. Not that God couldn't have healed me instantly, but he can also heal through other means.

Healing is a mystery which we may never fully understand until we see Jesus. I'm sure it will be one of the top questions we all ask when we reach eternity. I now believe I was following a trend and not the voice of the Spirit. That being said, my heart was in the right place, but my thinking was not. We need to hear a clear Word from God in regard to our health and let the Spirit deal with each situation according to God's will and plan.

## DIAGNOSIS AND SURGERY

When I first went to the doctors, their immediate diagnosis was asthma, so they gave me an inhaler to use for a couple of weeks. Of course, this did not work. When I went back they decided to perform a Bronchoscopy which revealed I had a possible tumor on my right lung.

I loved to sing ever since I was a child. The thought of possibly having lung cancer threw me for a loop.

Hearing the "C" word is such a frightening thing. The first reaction is, "Oh, no! I'm going to die!"

Then you recall the horrible stories about the side effects of chemo and radiation and wonder how you could ever make it through such an ordeal. I was only thirty-two at the time—who gets lung cancer at age thirty-two when they have never smoked? After all, I had already gone through the tragedy of losing my child and now this?! It just didn't seem fair. But after scopes, MRI's and PET scans it was revealed that I indeed had a mass on my right lung.

Surgery was scheduled and I was to have the tumor removed at the end of October. My doctor reassured me that it was not cancer and that I would be fine.

Following surgery, the doctor came to let me know that they removed two-thirds of my right lung and that it indeed was a cancerous mass. He said he would let me know when they would start chemo or radiation. I cried to God. I felt that I'd rather die than go through the physical trial of cancer treatment.

## A VISION

After a week of being in the hospital, I had to have the wound reopened because it was not clotting. I ended up being in intensive care for an additional week. I was on medication for pain. During this time, on one particular night, I had a vision.

It was the second week in the ICU and I was miserable and feeling abandoned by God. *"How could He let this happen? Where are you God?"* are some of the thoughts I struggled with. One night, above my bed, I saw the Lord on one side of me and the devil on the other. The devil told God, "I'm taking her life." Then God told him "NO." They went back and forth and it seemed so real, it was the strangest thing, watching the two of them argue my fate. Many may say it was a hallucination from the drugs, but for me it was real—like viewing a movie. In the end, the Lord spoke to me and said that I would not die, but overcome. He even reminded me of the scripture that says:

> *"I shall not die, but live, And declare the works of the LORD."* Psalm 118:17 (NKJV)

It was a rough two weeks in the ICU and I felt like I was going to die, but now I had a promise to firmly stand on. The promise that the Lord gave me was imbedded deep in my soul. "You shall not die!" This helped sustain me through all of the pain and the emotional hurt.

In the meantime, my husband was given a Word that the devil was trying to take off his right arm. That right arm was me and people rallied with him and held up his arms. They believed that God was going to do a miracle and that I would be okay and back at his side in no time. Many times we don't see the seriousness of doing the Lord's work and how vulnerable we can be to the wiles of the enemy.

The real tragedy was that several families from our church decided to leave because they felt my faith was "too small." Here I was, the pastor's wife stricken with this horrible disease and instead of rallying around a stricken warrior they leave the battlefield!

Why we kick the wounded is something I will never understand. I've learned from having been through this that it's all part of our journey in making us a better servant of God. My present pastor, Dave Hess, gave the following analogy in one of his sermons:

"Do we want a beautiful tree on the outside, or do we want to be pruned to bear fruit?"

Sometimes just being a beautiful tree on the outside seems tempting, but in my heart I knew that I wanted to bear fruit—so I chose to forgive those who judged me for "too small" a faith.

At the end of the day the question that still remains is "Why? Why cancer?" That's a question that I believe cannot be answered. Sometimes bad things happen to good people and only God knows the reason for our suffering and our infirmities.

## HEALING FROM GOD

My initial feeling when I found out the mass was cancerous was as if God had slapped me across the face, yet again. I guess it was disappointment and hurt. I don't know, but it wasn't long till I came to the realization that God did heal me. He let me live! I needed to quit blaming Him for the bad things in my life and I also needed to quit blaming myself. I grew up in a church that believed God is ready to slap you down if you're not perfect. That becomes your mindset and it's difficult to change it. I finally got to the place where I could grab hold of the grace and love of God, for His love is pure and never-ending.

In many ways, I experienced remarkable healing from God. Although the mass turned out to be cancerous, I was told that they had removed all of it and that no chemo or radiation was necessary. This was a major blessing for me. I only had to have check-ups for the next five years in order to make sure the cancer had not returned. That seemed like a walk in the park in comparison to the alternative. I was truly thankful for the outcome.

*"I will praise You, O LORD, with my whole heart; I will tell of all Your marvelous works. I will be glad and rejoice in You; I will sing praise to Your name, O Most High."* Psalm 9:1-2 (NKJV)

## PURE LOVE

How foolish we are to believe that God, who first loved us, could be so cruel as to put such a thing as cancer in our bodies in order to teach us a lesson. God is pure love and I think it's hard for us to grasp that concept because we don't fully understand what *pure love* is. Most of our love seems to be conditional, where His is not.

We all want to exemplify the pure love of God. That is what we strive for in our walk with Christ. When I was a kid, I always tried to be the "perfect" child. I always wanted to please everyone in the worst way, and yet I failed. To this day, my brothers call me—in a teasing way—"The Golden Girl."

We are all golden in the sight of our Creator. David reveals himself in the book of Psalms as not the most righteous man on earth and yet again he was the apple of God's eye. I truly believe that unforgiveness, ill feelings towards someone, any kind of stress or uneasiness can make you susceptible to getting cancer or many other forms of illness. Proverbs 4:20-22 (KJV) says:

> *"My son, attend to my words; incline thine ear unto my sayings. Let them not depart from thine eyes; keep them in the midst of thine heart. For they are life unto those that find them, and health to all their flesh."*

In Proverbs 17:22 (NLT) we read:

*"A cheerful heart is good medicine, but a broken spirit saps a person's strength."*

## A HEALED RELATIONSHIP

I feel my bout with cancer came through a very rough patch with my mom, who is very near and dear to me. We had a falling out about a year or two before we both became sick. We were burdened by a sour relationship and didn't speak for six months. She ended up with pneumonia and I with lung cancer.

My mom and I have a wonderful rapport, not just because we are mother and daughter, but because we are good friends. I am grateful that we were able to overcome our differences and resume the relationship that we formally enjoyed. Today, our friendship is different—in a good way. We can now convey our feelings without fear of losing each other's trust and love. Mothers are such a blessing when you are a child, but having them as a friend when you're an adult is amazing.

## SINGING

Many years have gone by and through that time, I was able to lead worship and sing in a women's acapella group for twenty-two years.

I decided not to let the devil win by taking my joy of singing. In the ensuing years, I never again had an issue with cancer, only a scar as evidence of my miracle from the Lord. Again, one of my favorite verses comes to mind—Psalm 30:11-12 (NKJV):

*"You have turned for me my mourning into dancing; You have put off my sackcloth and clothed me with gladness, To the end that my glory may sing praise to You and not be silent. O LORD my God, I will give thanks to You forever."*

I am very grateful for the healing that God bestowed on me. Although it may not be the instantaneous miraculous healing that we read about in the scriptures, it was still a miracle of God's intervention for me. I may not have been restored at a service held by a famous faith-healer, but it was definitely God who made a way of escape. I was so thankful to just be alive.

# 4

## Forgiveness is Mine

It was 1987 and the church was flourishing. Rick and I were having a wonderful time serving God and enjoying life. We had a great group of friends and relished worship, serving and just plain having fun together. My cancer was gone. The Lord had done a healing, not only in my body, but in my soul as well. I was singing again and one of my close friends and I were leading worship and doing musicals and pageantry in the church, which I absolutely loved.

It was so good to have close women friends. We would pray together, cry together, and laugh till we wet our pants. There's nothing more satisfying in a woman's life than to have other women she can share her heart with. I didn't have a sister so having trustworthy women companions was an amazing joy for me. Proverbs 27:9 (NLT) says:

*"The heartfelt counsel of a friend is as sweet as perfume and incense."*

## FRIENDSHIPS

My one friend and I had a wallpapering business for seven years; we were like sisters. We "got" each other. Sometimes there are just people in your life you really connect with. You laugh at the same dumb things and just have a great time together. We were best friends for more than ten years. The sisterhood we shared was such a blessing.

Did you ever have a time in your life where you thought, "Wow! Life is so much fun and satisfying it's almost scary"? That may sound funny, but I was saying to myself, "I hope these friendships, we have now, last forever." We had three other couples that we were close to and we always had a blast hanging out. Our kids were young and growing up together. They were forming their friendships with one another and life was sweet.

After seven years of wall papering, I decided to call it quits. It was hard on the knees and the money wasn't worth the pain. I was offered a job at a radio station where one of my friends was the sales manager. My best friend was disappointed, but understood my need to move on. We still spent time together, working in the church and doing our music. In fact, we even wrote a couple of jingles for local businesses and sold them.

## BETRAYAL

Though I was working full-time at the radio station, I still had my responsibilities at the church. My husband seemed happy with me working another job and gave me his blessing. However, after a while, he was starting to act a little strange. It seemed as though he was withdrawing emotionally from me and there was a growing distance between us. I thought maybe he was going through something spiritual or he didn't want me working at the station anymore. We talked about it and he never admitted there was a problem. I even cut back to a part-time position because I thought it may have been too much with all the responsibilities at the church.

Rick and I didn't argue much. We usually talked things over and tried to resolve our differences, but for some reason, we just weren't communicating well. I remember one night I ended up sleeping on the couch. Neither one of us had ever done this in our sixteen years of marriage.

One evening, in the middle of the night, I woke up. The Lord had revealed to me that there was something going on between my best friend and my husband. After wrestling in my mind, wondering what to do, I decided to write him a letter and plain out ask him if anything was going on. The next morning I gave him the letter and headed for my job. I was in anguish all day until I got home. I was afraid to confront Rick with the issue, but I knew in my heart that this was exactly what I needed to do.

As we talked, he admitted to me that something was going on and that he and my best friend were having an affair. He told me that they never consummated their affair, but that he had feelings for her, and her for him. It was like an arrow shot through my heart. To be betrayed, not only by my husband who I never would have dreamed would betray me, but to have a trusted friend—one I considered a sister deceive me, was totally devastating. What do you do? What do you say? I was completely speechless. Two people that I dearly loved and trusted had betrayed me.

I immediately packed some clothes for myself and the kids and went to stay with our friends to give me time to think about what to do. I felt so hurt, devastated, and disgusted by both of them. I spent many hours in tears, yet trying to not let my children see my hurt. They were already confused by what was happening and I'm sure wondering why we were staying with our other friends. Fortunately, they were happy to be hanging out with their close buddies so it helped deter other questions.

After two days of wailing and crying out to God, the Lord spoke to me. He simply said, "Go get your husband." *What God?* He said again, "Go get your husband." So I got up, got dressed, and went over to my best friend's house hoping they would both be there. There is one thing about God that we know is true and that is if He makes a plan, He is sure to work out every detail.

When I arrived at her home they were both there. Her husband was at work and she and Rick were talking in the kitchen. I walked in and God gave me so much boldness and strength. I was like a tiger protecting her cubs—protecting her family. I told them that they weren't in love and that what they were doing was ridiculous and foolish. I told Rick he needed to come home and be with his wife and family. At that moment the strangest thing happened, he came home!

Many have asked, "Why would you take him back? He betrayed you and was planning on making a new life with this women. What were you thinking?" I was thinking how devastating it would be for our children. I was thinking we've gone through so much in our life and have overcome so much that I wasn't willing to let that end over an irrational mistake. I loved him and I knew he loved me. I wasn't going to let it end if I could help it. If I had approached him and he rejected me, then I would have my answer. It would be on his lap, his decision and not mine. I knew in my heart that this is what the Lord wanted me to do. It was one of the hardest things that I have ever done, but God gave me grace to do it.

## CONSEQUENCES

The weeks following Rick's return to our family were extremely difficult. He was feeling guilty and I wasn't feeling very gracious. I made a conscious choice to forgive him, but it didn't mean all was well. My choice was based on the fact that he had confessed his sin and wanted to turn from it. It didn't mean that everything was warm and fuzzy. This kind of forgiveness takes time to manifest—to have healing and gain trust again. Unfortunately, we are not like our Father who is all forgiving. His grace towards us is astonishing. We knowingly betray Him on a daily basis, yet He is always ready and willing to forgive the moment we ask.

The other difficult part of this whole disaster is that the group of friends with whom we were so close with decided to leave the church. We understood this, but naturally felt abandoned. It was so hard and very heartbreaking. When you lose someone in your life, whether through death or loss of a friendship, you grieve. We were grieving. Of course, Rick was blaming himself and I was trying not to blame him.

Unfortunately, there are consequences to all sin and the ramifications to *this* sin were spilling out into my life, as well as Rick's. I didn't like it one bit, but there was nothing that could be done to change the situation. I was angry, and yet I was trying to have forgiveness for this man that I had loved for sixteen years. The fact that the man that I had gone through so many heartbreaking events with could so easily betray me seemed unbelievable. How in the world could he have allowed this to happen? What did I do to the two of them that would make them hurt me in this way? Was it my fault?

## LETTING OUR GUARD DOWN

I have come to realize that God allows people to come in and out of our lives, even if it's for a season. I do believe that people are removed from our lives because we are possibly holding each other back from doing what God has truly called us to do. I think our group of loving friends became so co-dependent on each other that we may have let our guard down against the enemy.

David experienced this in 2 Samuel 11:1 (NASB):

*"Then it happened in the spring, at the time when kings go out to battle, that David sent Joab and his servants with him and all Israel, and they destroyed the sons of Ammon and besieged Rabbah. But David stayed at Jerusalem."*

There was a battle going on and David sent out troops to destroy the enemy. The Kings of Israel went with the troops to fight, but this time David was taking a vacation from war. It was then that David committed his sin of adultery with Bathsheba, which in turn led to murder. He surely "let his guard down." These are the times when the enemy enjoys attacking the children of God and who best to use in destroying the church, but the pastor?

## PICKING UP THE PIECES

Our biggest fear was that others, out of our circle of close friends, would find out and leave our congregation as well. I have seen it many times, when a pastor falls, people flee. Fortunately, our church for the most part stayed intact. I'm not sure who knew or didn't know, but I was grateful to God for salvaging everything we had worked so hard to build.

As for my friendships, my heart was broken, but the Lord was there to pick up the pieces. In some ways, I felt more hurt by my friend than by my husband. I think the bond between women is sacred and you form a trust that makes you sisters in Christ. In fact, this woman was the one who spoke into my life concerning the mass on my lung. When that trust is broken, the friendship ends. I needed to forgive her, and I did, but our lives took different paths.

## GRATEFUL

God gave us beautiful friendships in the following years. These were friendships that we cherished and one's that had supported us in our endeavor to serve the Lord. He even brought one of the couple's that left the church back into my life many years later. I am grateful for all the people that God has put in, and taken out of our lives. It makes us who we are today and helps us realize that our full confidence can only be in our Savior. While we trust people, we still must keep our relationships pure and clean and only then can we view our friendships as "…sweet as perfume and incense."

The reason for this chapter is not to air our dirty laundry, but it is to help people understand that it is possible to experience a significant betrayal in your marriage and still survive and continue to have a loving and meaningful relationship. I never regretted fighting for my marriage because I felt it was the right thing to do. I am a person who, through the grace of God, was able to forgive and move forward.

Although, this time was extremely hard. I think the key to my ability to forgive was Rick's willingness to turn away from his sin and genuinely ask for mercy. Despite the fact that I had forgiven him, he had a very difficult time forgiving himself. He would bring it up in the following years. My reply would always be—"Honey, you need to let it go." I'm not sure he ever did.

# 5

## From House to Houseparents

We continued on with our ministry and enjoyed our new found friends. We had planned a cruise with a couple in the church and were on our way to the ship when Rick got a phone call from a Christian television station, Cornerstone TeleVision (CTV), out of Pittsburgh. They asked him if he would be interested in managing their sister station

**On our cruise vacation.**

in Altoona, Pennsylvania where we were living at the time. The time away on the cruise gave us a chance to pray about the offer and hear the voice of the Lord.

During our vacation, our friends Bonny and Steve encouraged him to consider the opportunity. They felt he would do a great job and they thought it was something he would enjoy. He had been on the local program many times before and seemed very comfortable and capable.

By the time we got home, Rick was pretty sure that he would accept the position, barring any obstacles that might interfere with the church. After discussing the details with the television station he accepted and within weeks started his new career.

## GETTING TOGETHER

It was an exciting time for both of us. His job consisted of managing the station, hosting, and producing shows for the Altoona area. He occasionally traveled to Pittsburgh to co-host their telethons. It was always fun because I got to go along and stay in a beautiful hotel. It gave us a nice time away from our everyday schedule. I also enjoyed meeting different people and learning how a television program is produced.

The CTV truck would arrive in Altoona about every six weeks to tape six shows called *Getting Together*. It was a hectic time, but we were both having fun using our creative juices. He was a fabulous host and was great at putting the shows together. I helped by doing a five-minute segment on the show called *Ponderings*. It was a wonderful experience for both of us.

The financial benefit of having the job at CTV was phenomenal. We worked hard and got completely out of debt. Rick didn't like being in any kind of debt and he didn't want the church to be in debt either. He was a very wise person when it came to finances and it made me always feel safe. This was one of the many things I appreciated about him.

He continued to work at Cornerstone for the next seven years and although things were going well we were starting to feel a tug to move on.

## A NEW JOB

One day he received a flyer in the mail. It was from a residential school recruiting students. The school was for underprivileged children and offered them a beautiful home and education at no cost. While on the website, he saw an ad for a house parenting position. He immediately said, "I found our next job!" As he told me about the position, I was a little apprehensive. We agreed that it might be something we could do within the next five years. I couldn't imagine taking care of ten or more children, but if that's what God wanted, that would be okay.

To my surprise, within the next year we had applied to the school and were hired. We approached most of the people in the church personally to let them know of our plans. They were very sad, making it extremely difficult for us to say goodbye. We had served the church for seventeen years and put our hearts and souls into the ministry. For some, it was hard to understand why we would transition from being pastors, but we felt we were moving on to minister in a different way...to children.

There were many things to do as we prepared to shift to our next calling in life. Our first order of business was to find a pastor for our church. We felt an obligation to see that they had a strong leader to continue the work. After much prayer and consideration, we found someone who we thought would be a good fit. It lifted a huge burden off our hearts and made us feel comfortable to continue with our plans. With this burden lifted there still was the selling of a house, packing, and mentally preparing. We had grown to love and appreciate our friends and congregants; it was hard to say goodbye. It was a bittersweet, exciting time.

## HOUSEPARENTS

Rick and I and our little red poodle Punkin moved to our new job in June 2001. When we arrived, a whole new world opened up to us. We went through the training classes and were then sent out to begin our work with the children. There were no student homes open at the time so we spent our hours going from house to house caring for the students. Just about every other day we moved on to another home, sleeping in different beds each night. It was a difficult process, but was required at the time. Rick was feeling displaced and uneasy. I remember him telling me that he felt like a nobody and disrespected. In Altoona, he had become known and respected in the Christian community. And was, to some extent, his own boss. Being under constant supervision and scrutiny was a little unsettling for him. By December of that year, we were finally placed in our own home with little girls.

For the next six years, we cared for ten little girls ages five through eleven. It wasn't an easy job, but we were good at organization and were structured so it helped things to run smoothly. We made a good team, although Rick was much more lenient than I. At times, we would have conflicts as to how things should be done. It was no different than raising your own children. We worked through our differences and were considered valuable houseparents.

Because we were taking care of girls, a lot of the responsibility for their care was put on me. I was starting to feel tired and drained. It could be emotionally and physically exhausting at times. That being said, Rick was a wonderful, caring houseparent. He played with the kids, prayed with them, and did most of the office work. He was a wonderful father to these children. I remember him speaking positive affirmations over one of the girls who was constantly down on herself. "You are 'somebody,'" Rick would tell her. He always made her feel accepted and loved. He truly loved the children and wanted them to succeed. Through our prayers and our witness, we believed they would come to know Christ as we knew him. After all, this was our ministry, our calling. Matthew 18:10 (NASB) says:

> *"See that you do not despise one of these little ones, for I say to you that their angels in heaven continually see the face of My Father who is in heaven."*

## THE TRAINING PROGRAM

The school decided to create a different training program for all the new house parents who were hired. They determined that hiring seasoned house parent couples to do the training would be the smart route to take. I asked Rick if we could apply. I thought it would be a good opportunity to help the newly hired house parents adjust to their new surroundings. We knew how hard a transition it was for us, so helping them would be a blessing to both us and them. Rick was not thrilled with the idea, but he knew that I needed a break, and so he agreed to apply for the position. Our chances were slim because many of the house parents needed a break and they too also submitted applications for the position. Rick was sure that we would be turned down, but he totally supported my desire to be a trainer.

Lo and behold, we were hired! Though we missed working hands-on with the kids, we still got to meet students from middle school and high school—a nice change. Our job was enjoyable and challenging in a different way. We no longer lived with children, but were able to pop in and see the kids whenever we wanted. They placed us in an off-campus house and we settled in without any problem. We were relishing our fun, new career.

## THE SUPERVISOR

It wasn't long before the honeymoon was over for the training team. Our supervisor started pitting the training couples against one another and playing favorites. Unfortunately, we were not one of those favorites. He was a very controlling and manipulative person, so it made the job very difficult and unpleasant. He especially didn't seem to like Rick or me very much either. We were never sure why. We were always conscientious about our job and the new house parents we supervised seemed to like us too. Things progressively got worse and we were feeling on the "outs." Even our training colleagues were treating us differently, at least we thought so. We were both becoming flustered and unsure what was going to happen. Was this man going to try and fire us? What would the future hold?

Our supervisor decided to take a six month sabbatical and we couldn't have been happier. Things were going well, but Rick was feeling unsure about our future. He thought maybe this man was planning on firing us when he returned. I told Rick that our supervisor had no grounds to stand on and not to worry. We prayed and asked the Lord for guidance and Rick felt like we should return to being house parents. I wasn't thrilled about the prospect, but since I did have a reprieve from being a house mom, maybe I could appreciate the job again. I needed to trust that we were making the right decision.

It was just short of two years since we started the training job, but if that was where God wanted us then everything would be okay. I didn't like seeing my husband so unhappy and feeling so unappreciated. He knew how much work the girls were for me, so he told me he would ask if we could be placed in a boy's home so he could do the majority of the hands on work. I was happy with that decision and so we asked our supervisors if that would be a possibility. They agreed, but requested that we stay in the training position until the end of the school year.

That was also when our boss was to return from his sabbatical. It all seemed to be working out well and Rick was pleased.

My husband had a particularly hard time being in a situation where he felt bullied. He detested bullying because he was bullied as a child. Though he was good looking and capable, he always seemed to feel like the underdog. In many ways, this made him an insecure adult. Our boss made him feel extremely bad about himself and his performance; he couldn't wait to be liberated from his authority.

## CHANGING RELATIONSHIPS

Time was passing and things were going okay. It was around Christmas time and there were many festivities to attend and activities to plan as trainers. We worked alongside an older woman who had been at the school for over fifty years. She was a very demonstrative and outspoken person. She could be very crass, and if she didn't like someone she did not hesitate to express her feelings. We had a good relationship with her until all of a sudden, things changed. Rick was upset and bothered by this because she started treating us poorly. Nothing had happened or changed other than our leaving the training job to be house parents again. Maybe that just didn't sit well with her.

We found out after Christmas that she had invited the training department for a special dinner, but it did not include us. Rick was devastated by this. I was hurt, but not in the same way he was. He felt rejected. I told him he should have been glad we weren't invited and didn't have to listen to her criticize and put people down, although I knew that we were the ones she was probably berating that night. "Honey, it just doesn't matter," I told Rick. But, it mattered to him.

## HOUSEPARENTS AGAIN

In 2009, we set our sights on our future and were looking forward to being placed in a boy's home. We were starting to make plans by putting ideas together and outlining our individual responsibilities in the house. We always enjoyed working together as we had our whole married life. Rick had a new kick in his step and seemed cheerful about our new venture. He was happy that he would be able to do the bulk of the work and give me a break. He felt I had done enough in the last years and wanted to ease the workload on me. I was happy about that too.

Several weeks later we got a call from human resources. They wanted to see us because they had some news. We were elated, thinking they were going to tell us which student home we would be placed in for the following school year. At the meeting they related that two house parents had just been let go and that they would be placing us in that home. It was a girl's home. We left disappointed because our hearts were set on working with boys this time. I told Rick that it was okay and that I was willing and certainly able to do the job. I always believe that things happen for a reason. Maybe there was a child in that home that really needed us. After all, God knows better than we do. We agreed that it would be all right.

## FOREBODING

It was a week before we started our new position with the little girls. We were off work that weekend so we decided to take a drive to New York and see our daughter and the grandkids. My mom decided to go along and we had nice trip. I remember that Saturday night sitting around Megan's table playing games and laughing. Rick seemed to be having a great time and was enjoying the grandbabies.

On our way home, we were talking about the wonderful time we had and how delightful it was hanging out with the family. My mom made a comment that it seemed like Christmas because on Christmas, after the opening of gifts and food, we usually played games and had fun. Rick immediately made a statement that I didn't understand. "We won't be doing Christmas at our house next year." I was so taken back by this and feeling a little angry, I asked him what he meant. He calmly repeated his statement. "We won't be doing Christmas at our house next year." My next statement was, "I think we will." It was a long, uncomfortable ride home.

# 6

## Rick

We had just settled in our new Student Home. It seemed familiar and comfortable to me, but Rick was feeling regret about giving up the training job. For the next two weeks, he didn't eat much and said that he couldn't sleep. I suggested that he make an appointment with a doctor to see what was going on, but he refused saying, "I'll be okay." Although I never saw him quite like this, I was use to him being melancholy; therefore, I took him at his word.

It was confusing to me that he was moping around the house and not enjoying what he was doing. He enjoyed house parenting in the past. After all, it was his idea to return to the job. One day when he seemed distraught, I remember telling him, "Come on! Let's get with it; we can do this thing!" The training position had given us both a time of rest from working directly with the children so I was ready to tackle being a mom of ten little girls again. Working as a houseparent is a difficult and exhausting job, mentally and physically, but I was up for the task.

## A CHANGE OF MIND

It was Saturday afternoon, about two weeks after we were placed in the home. We had planned to take the kids roller skating that day. He asked if I would mind taking them. He was going to stay home and do some things around the house and have dinner ready for us when we returned.

When we arrived home, we all sat down and ate dinner. Afterwards, the girls went to take their showers and get ready for bed.

That evening, he made a phone call to a co-worker who was a fellow trainer and friend. I later found out that he told this friend that he had made two huge mistakes in his life and leaving the training position was one of them. After his conversation, he told me that his friend had suggested that we call the administration and see if we could get our training job back. I couldn't believe what I was hearing! We spent six months planning on going back to house parenting because of how we were being treated by our direct supervisor. He was now changing his mind again. I reminded him how he felt belittled by this person and how poorly he was treating us and the whole team.

I told Rick that I thought we would look foolish and unprofessional if we called the administrators and changed our minds; besides, both jobs were great and we were blessed to have either one. Nothing more was said.

After the children were tucked in bed and all was quiet, we sat down to relax and watch a movie on television. While we were watching the movie, one of our five-year-olds came out, unable to sleep. She sat with us until she was sleepy. As distraught as Rick seemed that night, he was very loving and gentle with this little child. He always played the "Good Cop" while I played the "Bad." He would always say that he would treat these children the way he would have wanted to be treated, had he been placed at the school. That was his philosophy.

At eleven o'clock, we went to bed. We said goodnight as usual, and he told me he would get up early and start breakfast for everyone.

## SUNDAY MORNING

The next morning the alarm clock went off around 7:00 am. It was a cold, but sunny March day. I got out of bed to join the commotion that usually occurred on a Sunday morning. When I got up, all was quiet. Rick was nowhere to be found and the kids were still asleep.

I woke the kids as usual. They began looking for their tights, whining because they couldn't find their hair brushes, and accusing others of taking their things. It was the normal Sunday morning chaos before leaving for chapel.

I looked out the window to see if our car was there, but it was gone so I figured he ran out for something. I continued our Sunday morning routine, thinking he would be back soon. Rick usually took the children to chapel. It was odd that he wasn't home getting ready. My husband was not the type of guy to be late for anything. He was a very responsible person; I couldn't imagine what he was doing. I called our cell phone a few times, but he didn't answer. I thought he had forgotten his tie or something from the other house and went to get it. Time passed and still no Rick. I knew I needed to get the kids to chapel so I loaded them in the van and headed out.

## FINDING RICK

When I got to the chapel I ran in and asked another houseparent if they could supervise the students so I could go look for Rick. He hadn't been sleeping well so I thought he might have gone to the other house to get some rest. I arrived at the house and saw our car. I didn't have a house key so I pounded on the door, but he didn't answer. "He really must be sound asleep," I thought to myself.

I decided, after knocking for a while and getting no response, I would get the ladder in the garage and go through the window. We did this one other time when we were locked out.

As I walked into the garage, I saw a sight that no human being should see. My husband was hanging and there below him was the ladder...It was lying on the floor beneath him. I ran out of the garage in terror. I remember screaming, not knowing what to do. Just then, my friend Karen who lived two doors up was coming towards my house. She and her husband Allen were our fellow trainers and he was the one who Rick had spoken to the night before. Allen had called Karen to come and check on me and make sure everything was okay. It was not okay. Nothing seemed like it would ever be "okay" again.

## SHOCK

I recall sitting on the ground, outside our home, bawling. Shortly after, a police car arrived and a policewoman tried her best to console me. A grief like that is something that is uncontrollable. You can't stop your head from shaking and your gut feels as though it's going to come out of your mouth.

They took me to our friend's house and I laid on the floor and moaned for what seemed like hours. People were trying to offer me something to drink, continually asking if I were okay. My reply was, "No! I'm not okay. My husband just killed himself!"

Not long after, they whisked me off to a doctor's office—everything was such a blur. I kept asking if Rick was dead, but I knew in my heart there was no way he could be alive. I remember thinking, *"How could this be? How could he do such an unspeakable act? How could a man who preached the Word with such conviction and power be so tormented?"* It all seemed unreal. Like an unbelievable bad dream.

## THE FUNERAL

After it happened, they were going to notify my daughter Megan. I insisted they not tell her how her dad died. I knew it would literally crush her. She was pregnant with her fourth child and I was afraid for her and the baby's health. I knew Megan deserved to know, I just didn't have the ability to think rationally. Nothing was rational about the whole event.

I recall the next few days feeling numb and paralyzed. The doctor had given me sedatives. You feel as though you exist, but you don't recall much and you don't really want to remember anything. When the kids and the rest of my family arrived, the school placed us in a nice student home to accommodate the whole family. People were bringing us food, coming to visit, and sharing their condolences, but I felt nothing. My life was over.

We discussed having a memorial service, but I decided against it. We settled on just a viewing for the family and close friends. I couldn't bear the thought of an open gathering...what would we say? I didn't want people to know what he had done.

I realized that it was impossible to keep such a secret, but it made sense not to have a service. My kids agreed out of respect for me; but to this day, I regret not celebrating all the wonderful accomplishments their dad achieved in his life. At the time, there was too much hurt and resentment.

I remember the grace I had at Elizabeth's funeral. I was able to greet people and accept their kind condolences. But now, with my husband's death, I just couldn't function. I remember trying to get in the casket with him. I wanted to be close and feel him.

So many people from the school wanted to share their condolences so we decided to have a reception line. We put a picture of Rick on a table and had a video playing, showing happier times. Over two hundred people came that day, but I just didn't want to reveal the cause of his death. I knew everyone knew, but they graciously acted as though they didn't. With suicide, there is such shame. I guess, I felt as though people would blame me. I felt embarrassed that the strong man I lived with for years was so weak. Although unnecessary, I spent my whole life wanting to make Rick look good. He could look good on his own. Trying to cover this up was an insurmountable feat.

## MY CHILDREN

My family stayed for about three weeks; it was so wonderful having them around. Nathan was in the

Army so we usually didn't see him very often. He is a man of few words, but the whole time during his visit he would frequently give me hugs that spoke volumes. At the time Megan lived in upstate New York and had a very busy life.

**Nathan and Megan.**

Her husband Myson and their three children accompanied her. I felt comforted and happy that they were both at my side.

On top of my own grief and hurt, my heart was completely broken for my children. Questions consumed me...How could he do this to his kids? He loved them and they loved and respected him in return. Why would he hurt them like this? What kind of testimony would this be to them, and anyone who knew Rick was a Christian? I felt so angry, especially when it came to protecting the feelings of my children.

When I went to the doctor's office a few days earlier, the first question he asked me was, "Do you feel like hurting yourself?" Personally, I would never consider hurting myself—not only for my children, but for my God who has given me life. I would never want to leave that kind of legacy and couldn't believe that their father would have wanted too.

## THE URNS

The day Nathan and his wife Kate were leaving for home was a horrendous time. The funeral home called to let me know that my husband's ashes were ready. We decided to stop on the way to the airport to pick up his remains. I was happy to have someone with me. I walked into the funeral parlor. They greeted me and asked how I was doing. I gave them a nonchalant sort of answer—not really wanting to reply, but being polite. "We'll be right with you" they said. They went to the back and came out with a big white bag. In it, were the three urns I had picked out days before. As I walked out the door, a stream of tears filled my eyes. Nathan embraced me and took the bag from my hand. He placed it in the trunk of his dad's car.

As we drove down the road towards the airport I started to sob uncontrollably. All I could think about was my husband being in that bag. He told me his desire was to be cremated when he passed, but the beauty of the urns did not make up for the unspeakable, ugly reality that I faced. My thought, as I picked out the urns, was how beautiful and yet manly they were. I envisioned it like something from a movie. I would put the urn on a mantle, beside a picture of Rick so that I could view it and remember our life together. It wasn't like that at all. Just the thought of it made me sick to my stomach. It was a very disturbing moment to say the least. I didn't want an urn on a mantle to look at. I just wanted my husband back.

## SAYING GOODBYE

I composed myself by the time we reached the airport. I was very sad that Nathan and Kate were leaving. Kate had been such a rock for me during those three weeks. She helped me do all those important details that needed to be done when a family member passes. Both of her parents were deceased. She was very knowledgeable about how to deal with the affairs that need to be dealt with after a death. I was in a funk, so she was a wonderful help in my time of need. I gave them each a hug and kiss and they were on their way. Megan had already left for New York with her husband and three little ones.

It was still hard for me to believe that Rick could take his life knowing that Megan was expecting. With the new grandbaby on the way, it made what he did so reprehensible. Now, it was my time to figure all this out...at least I thought so.

Corrie Ten Boom said, "There is no pit so deep that God's love is not deeper still." I had to keep that in the forefront of my mind.

# 7

## Friends Along the Way

A few days after the kids were gone I decided I didn't want the urns anymore. It sounds kind of crazy, but that's how I felt. I called the funeral home and boldly asked if I could return the urns and their content. I told them I didn't know what I was doing when I bought them and because of my grief, I wanted to return them. The man on the other end of the phone was very quiet and then calmly said, "I'm sorry Mrs. Nicely, but we can't do that." I can't imagine what this poor man must have thought. I'm sure it was not a question he was expecting, or for that matter, had ever been asked. Grief does funny things to a person. Later, as I thought about it, I had to laugh at myself and when I shared it with my friends they laughed too.

## BEAUTIFUL FRIENDS

The school had moved me into another house on campus and it was now time to be alone. The white bag was still in the back of the car. Megan didn't know what to do with her urn and Nathan had taken his. Two urns sat in the back of the Honda. I had no desire to use the car or remove the bag. One day, my friend Linda offered to take the bag out and put it in my safe. I agreed it was a wise idea. She suggested leaving the urns there until I decided what to do with them. That seemed like a sensible and reasonable solution to me. Linda was a good friend and accompanied me a year later to scatter Rick's ashes. He loved the ocean, so what better place than for the sea to receive the remains of my beloved.

*"Then they cried out to the* Lord *in their trouble, and He saved them out of their distresses. He brought them out of darkness and the shadow of death, and broke their chains in pieces."* Psalm 107:13-14 (NKJV)

I had two other beautiful friends, Jen and Jenna. They were younger than I, but so devoted to me during my widowhood. They set up meals to be sent each night and would come over and visit me when I was lonely. They made me laugh in the midst of my grief and they were there to hold my hand when I cried. I knew when the phone rang during dinner time that it was one of them checking to see if I had eaten. They cared about me and yearned to see my heart mended. Jen and Jenna practiced the scriptures where it says in James 1:27 (KJV):

> *"Pure religion and undefiled before God and the Father is this, To visit the fatherless and widows in their affliction, and to keep himself unspotted from the world."*

My mom came to stay with me as much as she could. During her stay, she would sleep next to me. It was very comforting because nighttime is when I experienced the most despair. It was nice to have her there at any hour of the day if I needed prayer or just a "mom" hug.

## ANXIETY

I was feeling great fear and a tremendous amount of anxiety during this time in my life. I hung on to the scriptures that God had given me. He saw me through each panic attack. Being a spirit-filled, born-again believer doesn't make you immune to fear and panic attacks. It was definitely a critical time in my life. I had so many questions with no answers and I was still suffering from PTSD (Post Traumatic Stress Disorder). I was going to counselors, trying to receive the healing I needed. I soon came to realize that grief is a process. If only God could reach down and give us instantaneous healing, but sometimes it just doesn't work that way. Still, I stood on His word of promise. Psalm 34: 17-18 (NIV) says:

> *"The righteous cry out, and the Lord hears them; he delivers them from all their troubles. The LORD is close to the brokenhearted and saves those who are crushed in spirit."*

## COMING FORTH AS GOLD

Recently, I heard a quote that is not profound, but it's true: "You must keep believing what you believed before." I was still that young girl who gave her life to the Lord at the age of thirteen and committed her life to serving God. That doesn't change because you go through a trial or live through a tragedy. I've had people tell me that they don't know how I kept my faith with everything I've gone through. My question to them is, "How do you NOT keep your faith? Who or what would you believe instead?" I was yearning to feel the love I had for the Lord before all this took place, but God seemed far from me. However, I knew I would come forth as gold.

*"But if I go to the east, he is not there; if I go to the west, I do not find him. When he is at work in the north, I do not see him; when he turns to the south, I catch no glimpse of him. But he knows the way that I take; when he has tested me, I will come forth as gold."* Job 23: 8-10 (NIV)

## FAMILY SUPPORT AND MAKING PLANS

In the midst of my grieving, my son-in-law Myson told me that God had spoken to him about moving his family to my area to be close to me. I was thrilled at the prospect, and that he would give up everything and move to help me through this tumultuous season in my life. I had no family living near me, at the time, so it was a true blessing. I am grateful to have a godly son-in-law. I regard him as my own son.

God was seeing me through trying times. I had to make a decision whether or not to stay at the school and continue working or move on. I was conflicted because all my friends were there and it was all I knew for eight years. As a house parent, it is school policy if one spouse dies, the surviving spouse must resign from his or her duties. My thought was to apply for a different job and stay where I felt at home and comfortable. That was my plan, and when I say that, I mean my plan, not *God's plan*.

## GETTING HELP

My fear and struggling continued during the stay in the little house they placed me in on campus. There is no reason that I shouldn't have felt safe, but I was fearful. I couldn't sit in my house without closing all of the blinds every night and checking the doors several times. I got a lump in my throat if I heard any noise or unusual sounds in the night. That may not seem strange to you, but I was generally not a fearful person. It got to the point that it affected my sleep and made me terribly anxious.

I was trying to abide in my faith by quoting scriptures about fear; I still was unable to conquer it. I knew I needed someone to help me through. My daughter's friend Pat, from our church, was on a ministry team that helped people through hard times. I made an appointment to see her. I recall how I was sobbing when I couldn't find her house and thinking, "Oh this poor woman, having to deal with me." After a few phone calls she came to retrieve me and we finally settled into our session.

We discussed a wide range of subjects that day. I told her about Rick and the many events that shaped my life. I shared my ideas about why Rick did what he did. I questioned if it was because of the death of his child? Was it his infidelity? Was it the job situation? Was it me? Was it everything combined? She was compassionate and listened intently as I wailed uncontrollably at times. I explained to her how I was feeling—that I couldn't overcome the terrible fear that was overwhelming me.

She then prayed and quoted the scripture Isaiah 40:11 (NIV):

*"He tends his flock like a shepherd: He gathers the lambs in his arms and carries them close to his heart; he gently leads those that have young."*

## THE VISION

As she quoted the scripture, she asked me to envision myself looking at the scene in the garage the day of Rick's death. She said to let the Lord reveal anything He wanted to reveal. It was a very emotional day for me and as she prayed for God to give me a vision, I received a vision that I will never forget. It centered on that fateful day in the garage.

I entered the garage and I saw my husband hanging there and Jesus was there beside him. I cried to Jesus, "Why didn't you help him!" Jesus said, "I wanted to help him, but I couldn't." He gently took me in his arms and shielded my eyes from this horrendous sight. I could almost feel the tender arms of Jesus surrounding me. I then said to him, "Is he with you?" He answered, "Yes, he's with me." Then Jesus lifted me up in his arms and carried me out of the garage to the end of the driveway. He then held me up to God as if I were a sacrifice. In that moment, the crippling fear left me. Yes, I experienced fear again, but not the kind of fear that debilitates you. It was a monumental day and another hurdle cleared in my journey of healing.

# 8

## Hope and Healing

I was grateful for the healing I received that day. I was confident that God would orchestrate every aspect of my recovery. Would I ever be the same person I was before? Probably not. My hope was that the numbness would soon disappear and that I would feel like a person again.

### PHYSICALLY HEALTHY AND SPIRITUALLY FED

Years earlier, after my bout with cancer, I researched how stress affects the body. After Rick's death, I made a decision to do all I could to stay healthy. I had massages regularly and I even tried acupuncture. Exercising was part of my routine and I ate as well as I could. I felt that I needed to take care of my body as well as my soul. In the past, I had dealt with depression so I wanted to make sure that it didn't engulf me.

I do remember sleeping a lot during the first year. I wasn't sure if it was my body saying to rest, or my mind needing a break from thinking about all that had happened.

I went to visit my friends, Cem and Sheila, at their home about five months after Rick's death. I don't remember much, but since then she has shared with me how worried they were for me. She was trying to get me to go places and do things, but all that I wanted to do was nap. I would sleep on her couch for hours at a time. Other than talking about the incident, I didn't say too much. The depression was showing and my joy was gone.

It was the first time I had seen this couple in ten years. How very kind of them to receive me into their home. They loved and took care of me. I visited them every year for the next four years and I'm happy to say, I only sleep at night and never on the couch! God used so many people to be part of my healing.

During those first few years I would wake in the middle of the night and feel so alone. The enemy kept telling me that my life was over and something terrible was going to happen. In my mind I struggled with casting down every stronghold, yet it continually haunted me. I would call my mom or my daughter and sob hysterically. They would immediately pray and it helped me regain my peace. 2 Corinthians 10:4 (NIV) says:

> *"The weapons we fight with are not the weapons of the world. On the contrary, they have divine power to demolish strongholds."*

I was very diligent about attending church and feeding my soul. Not that I always felt like going, but I did nonetheless. I knew from the scriptures, that hearing the Word of God would bring healing in my heart. James 1:25 (NIV) says:

> *"But whoever looks intently into the perfect law that gives freedom, and continues in it—not forgetting what they have heard, but doing it—they will be blessed in what they do."*

I wanted to feel blessed again, and I knew if I continued to seek Him that would come to pass. Though I was feeling numb, I was confident my grieving would diminish. I was thankful; my hope was in the Lord.

# 9

# The Road to Restoration

Suicide was never something that was on my radar. I never knew any Christians or family members who had committed suicide.

It's funny how the body of Christ can talk so freely about cancer or any other horrific disease, but we can't seem to speak on the topic of suicide. It's shameful and so ugly.

## CHRISTIANS AND SUICIDE

I do remember over the last few years, two church services where the pastor talked about Christianity and suicide. I think talking about it strips it of its power.

At the end of one of those services the pastor gave an alter call for anyone contemplating taking their life. People went forward for prayer and then everyone went home. My hope was that there was some kind of follow-up, but I was only a visitor that day. In Isaiah, the scripture talks about a spirit of heaviness:

> *"To console those who mourn in Zion, to give them beauty for ashes, the oil of joy for mourning, the garment of praise for the spirit of heaviness;..."* Isaiah 61:3 (NKJV)

It's my thinking that anyone feeling that morose and unhappy needs continued help. People have to know that they are dealing with an enemy who is filling their minds with thoughts of hopelessness and despair. They are in a battle and can benefit from the prayers of their fellow Christians by finding Godly counsel. My eyes were opened that day during the service as I watched a group of people step forward who were seeking God but still contemplating taking their own life. It literally blows my mind.

Through my experience, I've come to the conclusion that we as a church need to be more open about our feelings and not live behind a fake smile. We need to accept people as they are and help them through trying times without judging them.

I want to talk about someone who was so anointed, so vibrant. He loved and served the Lord and yet committed this awful act. His name is Rick Nicely. How could it happen? Even now I sometimes ask myself that question. But I feel if he could carry out such an ungodly act then any one of us are capable of the same.

Had I known his deepest thoughts or if he had shared them with me, we could have combated this with prayer and fasting—breaking him free from oppression and suicidal thoughts. It was his choice to carry that burden alone. Was it pride? Was he afraid to be so vulnerable? What was he thinking? Isaiah 58:6 (KJV) states:

> *"Is not this the fast that I have chosen? to loose the bands of wickedness, to undo the heavy burdens, and to let the oppressed go free, and that ye break every yoke?"*

## 1,000 QUESTIONS

Eventually, I came up with reasons why he would do such a thing. He didn't leave a note so I didn't have the satisfaction of him saying, "I love you, but I just can't go on." He didn't confess to being seriously ill, nor bearing the thought of me having to go through the hard time that would follow. Those are things that movies are made of and unfortunately, this was not a movie. No, no note, just a thousand questions with no answers.

I've speculated as to why. When suicide happens to someone you love your mind is circling the years of the life you've spent with them, trying to find answers. Was he still grieving his daughter Elizabeth? Did he still feel guilty about his affair with my best friend? Did he feel bullied and oppressed? Was his insecurity so deeply rooted that he couldn't deal with it anymore? Was it me; did I do something? I asked myself these questions again and again, but still no concrete resolution.

## EVERYONE HEALS IN THE THEIR OWN WAY

After Rick took his life, I was seeing a counselor that suggested I go to a suicide support group. My first reaction was, "No way! I don't want this to define who I am. I don't want to be known as the wife of someone who committed suicide!" I think we all want to believe that we have perfect little lives and perfect families. It was horrifying and embarrassing to have people think of me as a "suicide survivor."

After a few months, I agreed that it may be a good idea to meet with others going through the same situation. I went to the meeting. There were about ten people attending. Each one gave their story. I also shared the vision that the Lord gave me. It felt good to contribute to the group. Most of the tragedies were five to ten years past. I couldn't believe my ears. *Ten years!* All I could think was if I'm still sitting here in ten years grieving so intently, then what's the use! I was looking for hope, not sympathy. I never went back.

Everyone finds healing in their own way so I realized judging this group was wrong and unfair. It just wasn't for me. I remember a song that I heard on the radio that greatly ministered to me. It was a song written by the secular music group Lady Antebellum called *One Day You Will*.[1] It is not a Christian song, but the message spoke to my heart. To summarize, it speaks of the pain you walk through in this life and although you can't see it when you're in it—down the road the sun is shining...

This song gave me hope. It's exactly how I was feeling.

## HINDSIGHT

As I contemplated Rick's words and actions taken over those past few years, in hindsight, I can see his change in behavior. Although at the time, I felt the changes were because he was getting older, even though he was only fifty-five. I remember telling my daughter that we allowed him to act the way he did by using the excuse, "Oh, he's just becoming a grouchy old man," or by saying things like "That's just your dad." In reality he was slipping into depression and we didn't know. Although he was always a sort of melancholy person, he never had a problem with depression. He never took medication or gave any hint of wanting to see a doctor about it. He, at no time, admitted to any sort of despondency. He cared for me when I was going through bouts of hopelessness, and he remained strong.

After Rick's death, my mom wanted me to see some pictures that were taken at Christmastime—prior to his death. It was a real eye-opener. When I saw them I was stunned. He looked so forlorn, so sad. When you live with someone for so many years you don't see it. I was use to his moods, his lows and his highs. That was "just him," the man I loved for thirty-four years.

Always having to be on the go, busy, on Christian television, and standing in front of a congregation every week was difficult—especially for someone like Rick who was an introvert. It was the spirit of God that was working in his heart that made him come to life as he preached the Word of God. He had a tremendous gift to teach and preach and was truly anointed by God. He showed compassion and generosity to many.

## ACCOUNTABILITY

I'm convinced that accountability is a huge piece of the puzzle when it comes to our Christian walk. As quoted by our pastor, accountability is "someone in your life that discerns your talents and abilities and makes sure you don't lose your fire."

For years Rick had a good friend Steve with whom he would share things and confide in. Unfortunately, when we moved from Altoona, their relationship was different. They were still friends, but the distance changed the dynamics of their friendship. Steve was part of Rick's accountability.

He also had a group of pastor friends with whom he met and prayed with on a monthly basis. When we moved from Altoona, Rick never connected closely with other Christian men. He didn't have anyone that he felt he could confide in. I believe that left him vulnerable and open to the arrows of the enemy. We attended church or chapel every week, but it wasn't enough. First Thessalonians 5:11 (NIV) states:

> "Therefore encourage one another and build each other up, just as in fact you are doing."

We all need accountability in our life. We should desire people to surround us and support us. It's important to have someone in our lives to correct us, even confess to. James 5:16 (NIV) tells us:

> "Therefore confess your sins to each other and pray for each other so that you may be healed. The prayer of a righteous person is powerful and effective."

It's so much easier for women to make these connections and emotional ties. Men don't want to seem weak, nor have their feelings exposed. At least, my husband didn't. I think if he would have confided in someone and told them how he felt, he may still be alive today.

## PURSUED BY GOD

God has been so good to me and has done so much healing in my heart. When it all first occurred, I thought for sure I would be on the couch watching TV and eating bonbons for a very long time. Don't get me wrong, I had many times of despair and totally ate my share of chocolate.

I remember my daughter's concern about my spiritual well-being the first year after Rick's death. I simply told her that I'm going to do all I can—go to church, go to counseling, and cry out to God for healing, but don't expect me to feel anything. That was the condition of my soul. I wrongly thought my husband's suicide was the last slap on the face, the proverbial "three strikes, you're out!" I'm telling you this because although I felt that way, God never stopped pursuing me. He never gave up on me or left me. I had a history with my Savior that wasn't going to end because of another adversity in my life.

About six months after it happened, I was at a Sunday morning service and there was an alter call given for healing or hopelessness. I quickly ran up front hoping to receive a release of some kind of joy. My pastor, Dave Hess, came up to me and started to pray. Before he was done, he had a word that changed my thinking entirely.

He simply said, "The Lord told me that your life will not end in tragedy." You can't imagine the deliverance I felt that day. A burden was lifted and pure joy entered into my spirit. It was another step in the restoration of my soul.

## Endnote

1.  Lady Antebellum. "One Day You Will." By Scott, Kelley, Haywood, Clay Mills. *Lady Antebellum.* Capitol Nashville, 2008.
For full lyrics go to: http://www.azlyrics.com/lyrics/ladyantebellum/onedayyouwill.html

# 10

## Widowhood

As I worked through my healing and was beginning to feel like myself again, I realized that I was now "a widow". It's such an overwhelming feeling to have been married and a part of something so strong, so encompassing for so many years and then it's gone.

I've talked to many women, widows and divorced. The reaction to losing a spouse and the possibility of remarrying is usually summed up into two categories:

1. If I ever lost my husband, I would never remarry.

2. I enjoyed being married so much, I would hope to be married again.

I fell into the latter. I loved being married, every part of it. I enjoy the companionship that it brings. There is nothing nicer than waking up each morning knowing there is someone there to have coffee or just chat with. Not much has to be said, but the presence of the one you love is so comforting. I may be old fashioned, but it's reassuring knowing that there is a person who loves you and wants to take care of you. I realize and understand that for some women that didn't happen in their marriages. And although Rick and I went through many challenges, I felt a security that was undeniable.

## ACHE FOR A HUSBAND

How do you get through this difficult season? You literally put one foot in front of the other. Your mind races with thoughts of the past, good and bad. When you go to bed at night you ache for that person to be at your side. You realize why human sexuality is so sacred and so godly. It unites you as one and when it is gone, you feel the sting of true loneliness and wanting. We need to look at the intimacy and not the act of love and recognize that it could be gone in a fleeting moment. I cried many nights thinking…if only I could touch him once again. Yes, it sounds like a country song, but the real truth is that you feel a piece of you is gone and you'll never get it back. I remember that feeling when I lost our child. The scripture does say that Jesus will be your husband.

*"For thy Maker is thine husband; the Lord of hosts is his name;..."* Isaiah 54:5 (KJV)

Yes, Jesus is my husband and He was there to comfort me, but sometimes I needed my earthly husband to embrace me and say, "It will be alright." I have to admit that one of the comments that I didn't care for as a widow was, "Oh honey, let Jesus be your husband." They were trying to encourage and comfort me, but that particular remark wasn't comforting in the middle of so much grief and isolation.

In time, I came to realize that He certainly was my husband in many ways. It's all part of being a widow. Is it any wonder why God, in his infinite mercy and wisdom, placed these words in Scripture?

*"Father of the fatherless and protector of widows is God in his holy habitation."*

Psalm 68:5 (ESV)

I desperately needed that protection. I was lonely and at times felt forgotten, uncovered and vulnerable.

## CRYING OUT TO GOD

Loneliness is an awful thing. It comes from deep within and creates such emptiness in you. You learn to overcome, only by crying out to God, and sometimes you don't feel like it. I experienced many hours of feeling sorry for myself, dwelling on my rejection and crying myself to sleep. Only by the true grace of God was I able to wake up the next morning with a renewed sense of peace. This is a process that continued for several years. Its part of the process of grieving and that is what helps produce healing in your soul. Everyone is different and everyone grieves differently. This was my experience and I'm grateful that God brought me out of the pit I put myself in.

## KILLING A BIG BUG

I soon realized being a widow meant you must fend for yourself. I, like many women, do not like bugs. In fact, I hate bugs! When I saw a big nasty bug I would yell for my husband, "Hon! Come get this bug; it's creepy!" He would come to my rescue and of course make fun of me because the bug wasn't as big or as creepy as I perceived.

After Rick died it was quite an adjustment. I remember going to the bathroom one day and there on the window— right near the toilet—was a huge, appalling, beastly bug staring right at me. I am not telling a "fish tale." It was enormous…for a bug that is. The first words out of my mouth were, "Help me Jesus and give me courage!" I found a magazine, rolled it up, and approached the bug. As I got closer, I concluded that I needed a plan. It was necessary that I executed an exact shot. My fear was that the giant bug would sense my insecurity and fly at my face, attempting to take me down. I crept up on him and with one fell swoop, I hit it hard with my magazine. I knew I had to get him the first time or it would be curtains for me. As I pulled my arm back to swat, I cried to the Lord, "Rick's not here God! You need to get this one for me!" I gave a fast blow to this thing and it flew up in the air and did a one-eighty landing straight in the toilet. Lifting my foot, I flushed him. "Thank you Lord. You ARE my husbandman." I prayed aloud.

## COMPANIONSHIP

When Rick died our little dog Punkin was fifteen years old. She was a cute little red poodle with a mild temperament. It was a great blessing having her at my side. It was always so nice when I got home from work, she would be there to greet me with her wagging tail and big brown eyes. She was so excited to see me and I was grateful not to come home to an empty house. She had been a part of our family for a long time. It helped to have someone to snuggle with in the evenings. It's amazing the pleasure a little pet like her can give. If I was crying she would curl up beside me and look at me so sweetly. I believe she could sense the pain and anguish I felt. I also believe she was feeling a little of that pain as well. Two years went by, Punkin was seventeen years old and having health issues that led to her being put down. It's always hard when you lose a pet. For me, she represented another part of my life with Rick. They were my family.

I spent the next year pet free. In a way it was nice not having to take care of someone and worry about having to be home at a certain time. The loneliness was challenging, even though I had family and friends to support me during the day, in the evenings I felt alone.

In a weak moment I decided I needed a puppy, so I searched and found one I liked. He was a sweet, little red haired Bichon Poodle named Tucker. He became a companion, a new member of my family. Unlike my other dog, Tucker was feisty. He chewed furniture, woodwork, and anything he could sink his teeth into. What was I thinking? I realized, however, that his companionship outweighed the terror he was wreaking. He is now a very nice dog and I love him, but it took so much time and energy. The moral of the story is to never get a pet during major transitions in your life!

# DATING

It was only a few months after Rick's death that I began to think about wanting to meet someone. You may say, "That's too soon, what about the memories of your husband?" Yes, I missed and loved my husband, but there was disappointment...it almost felt like a divorce to me. He made the choice to leave me. He must not have loved me anymore. I'll just find someone who will love me and care for me. I didn't think these were unreasonable things to think when your husband takes his life.

The months that followed were still filled with grief, mixed with an eagerness to move on with my life. I didn't know it, but I was in no way, shape, or form ready for any kind of relationship.

I made dates through a Christian dating site and it was a disaster. Some of these "so-called" Christians weren't even the same person in the photo! I was very naïve at the time. I hadn't dated anyone except my husband in thirty-six years. With each date, I would call my daughter Megan to let her know where I was going. It was a complete role reversal. She became the mom and I became the child. She disliked my dating experiences. However, it wasn't because of her dad—she knew the hurt that he caused—but she didn't think I would be safe and recognized my inability to make clear choices. I remember worrying about her when she was dating and now she was nervous for me.

My loneliness was clouding my judgment. I kept searching and searching, but still no "Rick." That's the peculiar part of my search. I would say, "I definitely don't want someone who is melancholy. I want a fun loving, easy-going guy." Yet, each date wasn't like Rick and it made me miserable.

## A LIFE COACH

I started working with a Life Coach about two years after Rick's death. I needed a new start and thought it would be helpful. I received her name from a good friend and decided to give it a try. Edna, my new life coach was an inspiration and at times pushed me to my limit. It was good for me; she needed to do that. Edna insisted that I start to journal regularly. It was something that I was accustomed to, but not on a routine basis. I would write about my feelings, about disappointment and love, and cry out to God to bring someone into my life. I would plead with the Lord to give me answers as to why Rick would do such a thing to himself, me, and the family. It was a healing process and cathartic. Once, Edna wanted me to write why I was grateful to be alone. That was a hard one for me, but I managed to come up with a list:

- Quite time
- Can watch what I want on TV
- Can eat whatever time I choose
- Can go out when I want
- The house stays cleaner
- Can have people over when I want

Kind of a lame list, but that was my discovery at that point. Now, it makes me chuckle.

I was inspired to make gift baskets because I felt they were a thoughtful way to show appreciation. I would put baskets together as gifts for my friends; it was fun and satisfying. I decided I could start a little business and make my baskets for other people. My last name was Nicely, so I called my business "'Nicely' Done Baskets and Gifts." It was fun to be doing something creative. My coach encouraged me to market them and gave me ideas how to do it. Although my business didn't take off, it was a good experience that gave me joy in my journey of healing.

At the end of my sessions with my coach, she asked me to write down how I felt about myself and what success would look like to me. She wanted me to describe who I thought I was. Here is what I wrote in 2011:

- I am a person who is trying to overcome three major events in my life. Those events are the death of my daughter Elizabeth, surviving lung cancer, and the suicide of my husband of thirty-four years.

- I'm trying to not let these events define who I am. I'm trying to start a new, fresh life in 2011.

- I would love to be the funny, confident, independent woman I am told by others that I am. Sometimes I believe it, and sometimes I don't.

- I love God and I want to serve Him, but I don't know where to start or what to do anymore. I feel I can only do the small things like being kind, loving my family, and giving to others.

- I think I finally believe that no matter how many failures I have and will have, God still loves me.

- I am a woman who has a lot of love to give and my heart's desire, even longing, is to find a perfect life companion through marriage.

- I want to live a long and happy life with this person. I want to travel, eat dinner out, play with my grandchildren and have fun.

- I want to serve God and help those who have gone through similar situations in life. If I don't get to do this, all I've been through will seem to have been in vain. I don't think God's like that.

- I want to be successful in my weight loss program because I know that it makes me feel better about myself.

- I would love to make gift baskets and be able to market them. It's something I really enjoy doing.

- I want to see my grandchildren grow up to be godly, successful adults. I desire that both of my children have happy long lives with their spouses.

- I want my mom and dad to enjoy each other and live their final years in peace and prosperity.

- This would be success to me and it's how I want my life to be.

As time passed, I could see the hand of God in my life, even though I whined to Him continually about bringing someone into my world. One of my favorite scriptures was Ecclesiastes 4:9-10 (NASB) which says:

> *"Two are better than one because they have a good return for their labor. For if either of them falls, the one will lift up his companion. But woe to the one who falls when there is not another to lift him up."*

## GROWING CONFIDENCE

It seemed I had spent years being in the shadow of someone else. This of course is only my perception. First, it was my mom who is a beautiful, charismatic person to whom people are naturally drawn. I thought of myself as always being Deborah Botteicher's daughter.

Then I married a handsome, charismatic man, a pastor, who people loved and respected. I became Rick's wife," but I was never able to identify who I really was. Yes, I knew I was a child of God, saved and bought with Jesus' blood. I had my own personality and talents. My husband and I were one, and I felt that we were one in God's calling for our lives, so it didn't affect how God was using me. After being widowed, I needed to figure out who I was. I was alone and had to become my own person. I would pray, "God, how do you want to use me?" "What is my destiny?" There is a quote, "Sometimes the road of life takes an unexpected turn and you have no choice but to follow it, to end up in the place you are supposed to be."

It was hard to come to the place where I accepted that I had a destiny outside of my husband. As I started to anticipate what God's destiny was for me, my confidence level grew and I was able to see that I am Pam Nicely, a woman with a calling on her life. That was a true breakthrough for me.

# 11

## Finding Purpose

Now I can feel the true grace and peace of God in my life. I've gone through much healing and the questions about Rick's death, although not answered, no longer haunt me. Yes, I occasionally wonder what happened, but it doesn't generate the anxiety in my soul as it once did. Again, one of my favorite verses of encouragement: comes to mind.

> *"The righteous cry out, and the Lord hears them; he delivers them from all their troubles. The LORD is close to the brokenhearted and saves those who are crushed in spirit."*
>
> Psalm 34: 17-18 (NIV)

My spirit had been crushed, but God delivered me and did a work of redemption and restoration. A few years earlier I wouldn't have believed my deliverance was possible. Even when thinking about Rick's horrendous death, my heart is no longer broken and my mind is free. Through the power of the Spirit of God in me, I have been able to cast down every thought of that horrible day. People ask me, "How did you overcome that scene in the garage, when you found him?" The answer is, and I mean this sincerely, "Only by God's mercy." Had I chosen to not turn to God, I'm convinced that I still would be living in turmoil. I would still be haunted by all of those questions, finding no peace. My life would be totally different today and not in a good way. Isaiah 61:7 (NKJV) tells us:

> *"Instead of your shame you shall have double honor, and instead of confusion they shall rejoice in their portion. Therefore in their land they shall possess double; Everlasting joy shall be theirs."*

## RESTORED LIFE

I wonder, when I look back why I had shame. A synonym of *shame* is *mortification*. It's hard to express how mortified I was at Rick's actions. We were one and whatever he did, reflected on me. When you're married, you want people to think the best of your spouse. Along with that, you take on the terrible guilt and notion that maybe, in some way it could have been your fault. I am thrilled that God is restoring my life with double honor and my confusion over the reason he took his life has been stripped away.

> *"You have turned for me my mourning into dancing; You have put off my sackcloth and clothed me with gladness, to the end that my glory may sing praise to You and not be silent. O LORD my God, I will give thanks to You forever."* Psalm 30:11-12 (NKJV)

Where do I go from here? Of course, I was still praying fervently for a spouse, but decided my online searching was over. That being said, I always had my eyes and ears open to any prospects. Whether I would find him at church, the grocery store, or at work, I felt the Lord could bring someone into my life. After all, anything is possible with God.

## THE LEGACY, MEMORIES, AND LOVE

The purpose and passion in my life is my family. They supported me through such hard times and were there to help dry my tears. My daughter, at the time of her dad's death, had four children and yet she was a tower of strength. She had her own grieving to do, which is not easy being a mom of four young ones.

My heart ached to help her through her grief, but I just couldn't do it. I was too devastated and consumed in my own despair. I was unable to share in my son Nathan's grief. He was away serving our country.

I cried many tears for my children; my heart was literally crushed for them. Rick and I spent much of our child rearing days trying to protect our children from grievous events in their lives, but there was no protection from this.

I hated the legacy that their father left them and yet, there was nothing I could do to change it. I wanted their memories of their dad to be good ones. I wanted them to be able to brag to their children, grandchildren, nieces and nephews of his accomplishments and victories. I desired for them to be able to share the wonderful person he was, but his demise made it hard for me to believe that could be possible.

He was a wonderful person, but a man who was deceived by the devil and taken down a dark road to a destructive end. That doesn't negate all the admirable things he did in his life. The fact is he loved his kids immeasurably and always wanted what was best for them. I can't answer for them because I don't know their hearts, but I think they know he loved them. I believe their love for their father has not changed. He was a caring and generous man.

## A DIFFERENT PERSON

I in no way think Rick's suicide can be viewed in a positive light; however, his death has made me a different person, a better person. I have more character, empathy, and compassion. I remember a time when I would have responded to people's problems by saying, "Get over it." Mostly in a kidding way, but everyone knows that there is always part truth in our sarcasm. I think I was tired of people coming to us with the same struggles time after time and never doing anything to overcome them. I actually hate to admit it, but when we left the church to work at the residential school, the church folks got me a mug with the inscription "Get over it."

If I could count how many times I've whined and cried to my family and friends about not being able to find a mate, I would need a lot more fingers and toes. They had every right to say to me, "Get over it," but they didn't. They loved me through it, just as I've been learning to do with others. I also appreciated life more and spent more time enjoying it instead of thinking about it. I stopped thinking about all of the things I didn't have and focused on all the blessings that I did have.

I am very thankful that my children were adults when it happened. Although challenging even for an adult, a child is not able to process such heartache and could blame themselves for the actions of their parents—same as they do in a divorce.

## LENORA

My hairdresser Lenora's husband took his own life a couple of years after Rick's death. He was a handsome, charismatic man who seemed to have it all together. Lenora's children were teenagers when he died and it ripped them apart. Children's hearts are so tender and vulnerable. They had many obstacles to overcome and felt abandoned, especially her daughter who was only fifteen. I am happy to say that they are doing well and working through their feelings, but it's something that could possibly scar them for life and change their destiny. I think about them often and pray for their healing.

I was appreciative that I could be there for Lenora and help her through her unexpected time of grief. It's amazing how God brings people into your little world. I believe there is always a purpose behind every person who enters our lives. She's told me how grateful she is that we became friends, and I feel the same. We didn't know Rick's and Mike's—Lenora's husband—hearts and their true hurt. Only God knew that.

*"...man looks on the outward appearance, but the Lord looks on the heart."*

1 Samuel 16:7 (ESV)

## MOM AND DAD

My mom and dad didn't live near me when Rick passed away, but I remember the look in my dad's eyes when I first saw him after the incident. He's from the "Old School" were men don't cry, but I knew he was crying on the inside for me. My mom would come and stay with me and sleep in my bed when I was fearful. One day, she was visiting and I had an errand to run. When I got to the parking lot of the store I started to cry uncontrollably. I called her on the phone and told her that I couldn't do it anymore...I'm so lonely... what am I going to do? She encouraged me to come home so we could talk. I had similar emotions throughout my healing process and I was thankful she could be there for me. I remember one night, I was on the floor sobbing so heavily, I couldn't catch my breath. I heard her cries to God, "God help her, take away this grief." I was their child, and as I felt helpless with my own children, they were feeling that same helplessness for me.

## JOHN AND LOUISE

Rick had five sisters. In recent years, we had become closest with his sister Louise and her husband John. They would come and visit us on occasion and we always had a great time. Louise was a breast cancer survivor of fifteen years. She fought hard to beat the cancer that was trying to take her life. When Megan phoned to tell her about Rick, it paralyzed her. Her question undoubtedly was "Why?" It was difficult for her to understand Rick's motive. She was left with a deep emptiness in her life. She was trying to survive, and Rick couldn't face living. Each time she came and looked into the eyes of his grandchildren, her mind would start to ask that same haunting question. What would make him do such a devastating thing? I am pleased that they are still in my life and have been an immeasurable blessing to me and my children. Every time they visit they do something special for the grandkids. "We want to fill in the gap for their grandfather," they tell me. They most certainly have done that and I am thankful.

## MY HEART'S DESIRE

My heart's genuine desire is for God to use me to minister to people, especially women suffering loss.

I want people to know that no matter what you go through, you can still come out on top and still be in love with your Savior.

God spoke to me about three years after Rick's death and told me to write a book about my victories. I replied, "I'm not able to do that Lord, but if you want me to, you'll have to make a way." To me writing a book seemed as big a task as Moses being asked to free the Israelites. Though not quite as high a mission, writing books was not something I thought I could do.

I accepted that I must wait on God for the opportunity to fulfill this calling. I knew he would open that door when the time was right. I didn't consider myself a writer and couldn't do it by myself. It had to be inspired and directed by God and so it was with the printing of this book—Praise the Lord!

## SHARING MY STORY

In the meantime, I was honored to have the opportunity to speak at several women's events. At one event, I put together a *Basket of Hope* during my testimony. I shared my story and as I did, I added items to my basket. My testimony was entitled "From Loss to Hope." I related that when I lost my daughter Elizabeth, I lost a piece of my heart. Yes, God does heal our hearts, but after thirty some years

I still have that piece missing. Of course, the pain has subsided and I have fond memories of the time I had with her. She is still a part of me and always will be. I then placed a box of heart shaped chocolates in the basket to express that loss.

When I lost part of my lung, I felt as though I lost my song. I loved to sing and I believed that part of my life was over. I was wrong and God gave me years of using my voice in song. I put a Christian CD in to represent that song.

When I lost my husband, I lost my right arm. Rick was a very handy guy and could do just about anything with tools. I never had to worry about fixing anything around the house because he always had that covered. That was symbolized with a tool kit made especially for women. There were several other items in the basket that related to loss and how God had restored my life and gave me hope.

It was so freeing to be able to share my story. It was healing for me and I believe it can, and will be, healing for others. Suicide, in itself, is a very difficult subject to broach. I am passionate about discussing the subject because I feel that the Church in general is uncomfortable talking about it. I know, from my own experience, how difficult it can be to talk about.

## NOT KNOWING
## HOW TO RESPOND

I recall going to a counselor when it first occurred. At the time, I felt somewhat alienated from people because I sensed them steering away from me so they wouldn't have to face me and talk about how Rick died.

The counselor then shared how her father had taken his own life. When she told me, I hardly reacted; I didn't know what to say. When I left the session, I felt so ashamed that I hadn't acknowledged her loss. Here I was seeking help about suicide and I couldn't bring myself to talk to her about what happened in her life. I couldn't talk about the very thing that encompassed my life. It opened my eyes to see how other people feel when that kind of tragedy occurs. It almost makes you speechless, not knowing how to respond.

## SUICIDE AND THE
## END TIMES

In the end times I believe there will be more people tempted to end their lives. They may do this out of fear, or the feeling of hopelessness.

*"Men fainting from fear and the expectation of the things which are coming upon the world;*

*for the powers of the heavens will be shaken"*
Luke 21:26 (NASB)

It's difficult to watch the news these days and not experience a twinge of fear, but it's encouraging to know that our God is in control of our existence and that Jesus has already won that victory. We need to hold on to that promise, and with God's help, not let satan crush and destroy our lives. Psalms 91:4-6 (NIV) says:

*"He will cover you with his feathers, and under his wings you will find refuge; his faithfulness will be your shield and rampart. You will not fear the terror of night, nor the arrow that flies by day, nor the pestilence that stalks in the darkness, nor the plague that destroys at midday".*

I know my husband must have felt that hopelessness and let his guard down against the enemy. If I could only do a small part in helping people through desperate times, I would feel abundantly blessed.

# 12

## The Dress on the Tree

It was June 2013. I was enjoying activities in the church and single life wasn't so bad. I was working at the front desk of a chiropractor's office, interacting with a lot of people. Everyone that worked there was a Christians so it was a positive, encouraging atmosphere and a lot of fun.

Our church's annual June picnic was fast approaching. Besides lots of food and games, there was always a dessert contest. People brought in the most fabulous desserts. Some were so creative and beautiful and some just taste amazing. This year was no different and I offered to be on the committee to judge the desserts. What better committee to serve than one where you get to taste all the yummy sweets!

## DAVID

There were so many entries that year, but a winner had to be chosen. I was standing at the judging table when a gentleman came in with a beautiful white chocolate fruit torte. As he handed it to me, the woman I was standing with—knowing I was single—mentioned that he was single. She told me he was a very sweet man and that his wife had passed away a couple of years prior. His wife had suffered with cancer for a few years. She informed me what a wonderful, caring husband he had been to her. I didn't think too much about it and continued my job with the other judges.

When it was time to announce the winner, my daughter and I were standing side-by-side. They called all the winners to the stage and it so happened that this gentleman had won first place in the contest. They announced, "David Fleming is our first place winner with his delicious torte!" At that moment our pastor's wife Sheri and his good friend Joe yelled, "And...he's single!" Megan gave me a jab and whispered, "He's kind of cute." At that moment she yelled. "My mom's single!" Suddenly, his friend Joe turned around and introduced himself to my daughter and me. He then went over and grabbed Dave by the arm and practically dragged him to meet me. He then said to Dave, "I want to introduce you to my good friend…what's your name?" We had a good laugh!

As we stood there, we felt like two middle school kids meeting for the first time. We had an awkward conversation. He was a little shy and I don't think he knew what to say. I filled in the silence by babbling on about who knows what. We engaged in some small talk for a few minutes. I was thinking, "Wonder when he's going to take my number?" I couldn't stand it anymore so I said, "Would you like my number?" He fumbled with his phone and nervously said, "Sure." Behind us stood my daughter and his friend Joe with big grins on their faces.

A week passed and I still hadn't heard from Dave. I figured he wasn't interested, or possibly he was too timid to call. I was at the point where I knew if it was God he would call, but if not, that was okay. I had finally reached the place of peace about the whole matter.

A day later I got a phone call; it was him. "Would you like to meet for dinner?" We met for dinner and talked the whole time with no hesitations. It was like we were old friends. We continued meeting a few times a week and enjoyed each other's company.

# A YARD SALE
# WEDDING DRESS

About a week after we went out, I was out and about and I came across a yard sale. I'm not one to pass up a good sale. I was on the phone with a friend when I saw a beautiful dress hanging on a tree at the sale. I said to my friend, "Hey Brian, I've gotta go, I see my wedding dress hanging on a tree!" Of course, his reply was, "What?" I repeated, "My wedding dress is hanging on a tree, bye bye." I was just teasing; however, I thought I would check out the yard sale and see what other treasures they had.

As I wandered through tables and piles of "stuff," I was drawn back to the dress on the tree. I was thinking, "If I were to remarry, this is the kind of dress I would love to have." It was a gorgeous designer label dress. Cream colored with beautiful lace on the bottom, the top was an over the shoulder style, made of chiffon with a beautiful train down the back. It would be simple and perfect for a second wedding.

As I was checking it out, the gentleman manning the sale asked if I was interested in it. I inquired the price and he told me it was twenty dollars…twenty dollars. My wheels were turning. I thought to myself, I'm not getting married now so twenty dollars would be a waste of money. I didn't want to buy it just to hang it in my closet. I had enough unworn clothing as it was. I told him no thank you and that I didn't really need it.

I continued to inspect the other items at the sale and found a few things I could use. When I went to pay, the gentleman asked me again if I was interested in the dress. My reply was, "No, that should be worn for a wedding and I'm not even engaged." I did tell him how beautiful it was and that it was just my size. He then said to me, "If you buy a glass of lemonade from my little girls, I'll give you the dress for a dollar!" Now that's a deal I couldn't pass up, even if I never wore it!

I left there thinking how silly I was and that I would never get any use from this garment. I got home and decided to try it on to see how it looked. I put it on and it fit me to a "T." I felt like a princess in it. My daughter visited me the next day and I tried the dress on for her. She absolutely loved it and told me I looked like a bride. Too bad I wasn't getting married any time soon.

## WAITING ON GOD TOGETHER

As our dating continued, Dave and I talked about life and discussions were brought up about us possibly ending up together. It was never really clear that he was the one for me, or me for him. We were both just waiting on God to show us if we were to be together.

Dave was really different than my first husband. He was laid back and easy going. Nothing seemed

**Dave and I.**

to rattle him, and I liked that because I was tired of drama in my life. He told me the story of his wife's illness and how he took care of her. The tears in his eyes showed me that he was a man of compassion and a wonderful caregiver. When I revealed what had happened in my life, he took it in stride. It didn't seem to bother or rattle him. I had been on dates before and when I told them about my tragedy, they looked as though they wanted to run.

I had a list of characteristics that I wanted for a husband. I wanted my next marriage to last the rest of my life. It was important that God was the one who would bring us together. I certainly didn't want to make a mistake out of loneliness or discontent.

It's harder when you've been married for a long time to your first and only love. When you grow older, they seem the same to you, even though there is extra weight and maybe a few gray hairs. If you love them, you look at your spouse as if seeing them for the first time. At least, that was my experience. Rick was as handsome to me from the day I met him till the day he died. When you're dating as an older adult, you don't get the privilege of falling in love with a young, good looking man. That being said, Dave was a very attractive guy.

I wanted someone who I was attracted to, but most importantly had a close relationship with the Lord and held the same beliefs as me. It was important that we connected on that level. I enjoy laughing and having fun so it was essential that the man I marry could make me laugh. I needed more laughs in my life. Even the scripture says:

*"A happy heart is good medicine and a cheerful mind works healing, but a broken spirit dries up the bones"* Proverbs 17:22 (AMP)

I desired to have a person who wanted to take care of me and love me unconditionally. I think that's what most women want. It may sound silly, but I didn't want a "stinky" guy. My husband bordered on being compulsive about his hygiene, taking two showers a day, but that's what I was use to. I grew to appreciate it—especially after talking to other women who told me horror stories about their husband's cleanliness habits, or lack thereof.

## A PROPOSAL...OF SORTS

It was a few weeks after we met and Dave wanted to introduce me to his family. We went to his son's house for dinner one evening. After we ate, we were just chatting and Dave randomly said to his son, "What would you think if I told you we were getting married in October?" Everyone's jaw hit the ground, especially mine! His son looked stunned and didn't say a word. It was so uncomfortable. Even though Dave tried to make a joke out of the whole thing, the air was tense. It was then I realized that he was very interested in me.

Yes, I had my list, but God had his will for Dave and me. We were sitting on my couch one evening just talking and then out of his mouth came, "When do you want to get married?" No on the knee, big ring, I love you so much—all the things girls expect when someone asks them to marry them—just, "When do you want to get married?" It took me back because I wasn't really expecting it. I didn't recall him saying that he loved me or couldn't live without me. After all, we had only been seeing each other for about six weeks. This time, I was the one who was speechless! "Ahh...ahh...I've gotta think about it." He was very gracious and said, "Okay."

# NO DOUBT

There was no doubt in my mind that God had brought us together and we were both having strong feelings for each other. I prayed, "God, is he the one for me?" He seemed to be everything that I had asked God for. He was sweet, funny, and loved the Lord. He was probably one of the smartest guys I had ever met. My family thought he was great, even though they too had only known him for a short time. His mother was sweet and seemed happy that he had met someone.

His friends invited us out often for dinners and social activities. I think they wanted to make sure he wasn't getting involved with someone that wasn't right for him. It is nice that people care so much and want what's best for you. Everyone knew our stories and many had heard how we met at the church picnic, and were cheering us on. People enjoy a good love story.

Dave's daughter lives in Georgia so we planned a trip so that I could meet her and her family. It was to be an eleven hour trip, but turned out to be seventeen hours. There was a mudslide that buried the interstate. That detained us, not to mention the two automobile accidents that occurred on the alternate route. It gave us plenty of time to get to know each other more, which was a good thing. The time went so fast and we talked non-stop. During that trip, I told him that I accepted his proposal and now we just needed to make the decision as to when to tie the knot. We were both thinking that we were a little too old to drag this engagement out. On the other hand, if we got married soon, we may hear the backlash of people saying, "You really don't know each other."

As we prayed and thoughtfully considered our choices, we came up with the month of November, three months away. My thought was December, but I was overruled by him and my daughter who couldn't wait to see me married. They won that battle. We got busy and planned a wedding!

## SHARING THE NEWS

Now it was time to let the rest of our family know our plans. Some were thrilled and some not so much. His nineteen-year-old granddaughter sent him a text saying, "If I came home after seven weeks with someone and said I was getting married, my dad would kill me!" We understood how she felt and it was kind of refreshing seeing how much she cared about him.

As the wedding plans continued, everyone seemed to calm down and accepted the fact that God brought us together.

# THE WEDDING

November 2, 2013 was an absolutely gorgeous day, not one cloud in the sky. Friends and relatives traveled distances to attend; it was an exciting day. I think that people were feeling grateful to God and delighted how He brought us together. Sometimes, you're fortunate to find one person who loves you.

I felt blessed that the Lord granted me such a special guy to grow old with. He is truly a prince.

**Our wedding day.**

We invited about one hundred people to share our joyous occasion. As they arrived that weekend, it felt so good to be surrounded by everyone we loved. The last time I was with some of my friends was in the wake of my husband's death. Now it was time to celebrate. Isaiah 61:3 (NIV) says:

> *"And provide for those who grieve in Zion--to bestow on them a crown of beauty instead of ashes, the oil of gladness instead of mourning, and a garment of praise instead of a spirit of despair."*

I was thrilled that I was going to get to wear my "dress on the tree." Only paying a dollar for the

dress made it so much easier to spend quite a bit more on the shoes! Everything fell into place and we had a beautiful ceremony. Pastor Dave, who had earlier given me the word, "Your life will not end in tragedy," performed the ceremony. That indeed was a life changing word and now my life was changing again with a wonderful man. I was

**Dad and I, and my yard-sale wedding dress.**

looking forward to seeing what God had in store for both of us.

# 13

## Moving Forward

When I look at my life now, I realize how truly blessed I am. Had it not been for God's mercy and grace, it's hard to tell where my life would have led. As I reflect and see the hand of God on each circumstance, I am grateful that I made a choice to forgive myself, Rick, and God. I understand the choices we make in our lives, affect our future.

### DEALING WITH ADVERSITY

Many times I think about my daughter Elizabeth and wonder what would have become of her life. I also ponder the likelihood that if Rick and I would have kept bitterness in our hearts, we may have divorced. We would not have had our amazing daughter Megan, and the six beautiful grandchildren that I enjoy so much. It is exciting to dream about their future and the possibilities of their lives.

God was so merciful to me when I had my bout with cancer. I recall how angry I was with Him when I found out that I would lose my lung. I was like a child having a temper tantrum. How dare He allow this to happen after I just went through the death of a child? I actually said, "God, I already had my big trial, why this too. It's not fair?" How dare I stand before a holy God with rage. We live in a sinful world and are exposed to reprehensible situations. How we deal with the struggles in our life is completely up to us.

We reap what we sow by the reaction we have to adversity. We have the ability to sow good seed that will blossom into joy in the future. If we continue in arrogance then we prove to God that we don't trust Him. God is more interested in our actions than He is our words. I don't think He needs or wants an apology; I think He just wants us to ask forgiveness and then change.

In reference to my husband's indiscretion, I will never forget when God told me, "Go get your husband." I know that if I had not done what the Lord told me to do, Rick and I would have had no future. It would have affected my children's futures and the way they perceive marriage and relationships. I am pleased to say that both of my children are happily married. First Samuel 15:22 (NIV) says:

> *"...Does the Lord delight in burnt offerings and sacrifices as much as in obeying the Lord? To obey is better than sacrifice,..."*

I don't know the consequences that may have transpired at Altoona Full Gospel Church after the incident of betrayal. If Rick had decided to leave me or if I had chosen not to forgive, the outcome would have been completely different. That could have been the end of full time ministry for both of us. As for the church, God would have intervened and raised up someone to continue the work. It was His church, not ours.

## REMARRIAGE AND FORGIVENESS

I was honored to be able to work in church ministry for many years. After Rick's death, when I was thinking about remarrying, I said "Lord, if you want me to marry a preacher again, that would be okay, but if you don't, that would be great!" Had He chosen a pastor for me, I would have felt blessed. My new husband is not a preacher, but is a wonderful man of God. He is exactly the right person for me, and God's timing was perfect.

Concerning Rick's death, many have asked, "How did you forgive Rick for what he did?" When it first occurred, I was extremely angry and didn't consider forgiveness. I was overwhelmed with hurt and anger that consumed me. My heart was crushed and bruised, making it a challenge to think straight. I was conflicted about my feelings. On one hand, I had so much love for this person, and on the other, so much hostility. How can a Christian have hostility? Hostility is the state of bad feelings and I certainly was experiencing that. I am grateful that God knows our true heart and not just our hurt heart.

## EMPATHY

Through prayer, counseling, and time, the Lord gave me empathy for my husband. Empathy gives us the ability to understand and share the feelings of others; in turn, it gives us the desire to forgive. Sympathy is easy; it's just feeling sorry for someone. Although I felt sorry for Rick, my anger was more encompassing.

My first thoughts toward my husband were sadness. It was not only a loss to my family and me, but to everyone he came in contact with. We were now going to miss all the accomplishments that God meant for him to fulfill his destiny. He would never get a chance to see his beautiful grandchildren grow up and make their mark on the world. We would never grow old together and enjoy each other in our retirement. God gave Rick his life and it was not his to take. That is God's decision, not ours. We are not our own and we must remember there is always a reason to have hope.

Secondly, I became angry. Why would he do something so selfish? What kind of inconsiderate, self-centered person would even think about doing this to their family? Didn't he have a care for how we felt? I would scream at him, "How could you do this to us?" I would plead with God to take away my anger and let me see a clearer picture.

Later, I thought about what Rick was feeling on that day. Did he think about his kids? Did he try to talk himself out of it? Did he wake up that morning and say, "I'm going to kill myself today?" I tried to set aside all the preconceived notions I had about suicide. How it seemed so demonic or that only a crazy person would consider it. Then I thought how he must have been suffering in silence. He was trying to hide so much pain, pain that from my perspective may not have driven me to such an end, but it did for him. Things that weren't difficult for me may have been insurmountable to him. I tried to see his pain and suffering from his viewpoint and not mine.

Before I had empathy, I was wallowing in my own grief and anger. I was the one being selfish and judgmental. Just because you have empathy doesn't mean you condone the act, but it gives you the allowance to forgive. I realized too late that Rick needed help. Unfortunately, he didn't seek it.

## CHOOSING FORGIVENESS

I had to remember that he was the father of my children and think about the good times we spent together. There is a bond when you're married that lives on forever. God took away the hurt and disappointment in my life and gave me true forgiveness. What is true forgiveness? To me, it's saying "God, I choose to forgive this man. Lord, give me the spirit that follows that." We don't forgive on our own; we choose and then God does the work. We have no forgiveness without Him.

Of all the experiences I've had in my life so far, Rick dying of suicide was the most difficult—maybe, because it's the most recent. If I had made the choice to not forgive, I'm sure my life would have gone in a downward spiral. I would have been letting go of my faith and turning my back on God. Hebrew 10:26 (NIV) states:

*"If we deliberately keep on sinning after we have received the knowledge of the truth, no sacrifice for sins is left,..."*

The decisions we make in times of testing are important, important enough to change the destiny of our lives. Carl G. Jung quotes:

*"The difference between a good life and a bad life is how well you walk through the fire."*

I want to have a good life and experience all that the Lord has for me.

## A MEMORIAL SERVICE

While talking with a friend not long ago, he posed the question, "Would you consider having a funeral for your husband?" My first thought was, "It's too late," and then it came to me, he was a great man and deserves to be honored for all the wonderful things he accomplished in his life.

When I discussed it with my daughter, she had tears in her eyes. She expressed that she needed that closure, and would love to have a memorial for him. We are now working on a date for Rick's memorial service.

## ANGER, COMPLAINING AND PRAISE

Do you have anger towards God for something that has happened in your life? Have you held unforgiveness towards Him? In some ways, being angry with God means that you have formed a relationship with Him. Your anger is not a sign of disbelief or denial of God. You're comfortable in expressing your feelings because you have a history with your Savior. Is it right to be angry with Him? No, but if we're feeling angry, we should confess it to God and ask His forgiveness. He already knows your thoughts and your heart and loves to forgive.

Every time David from the Bible expressed complaints toward God, he ended up praising Him. That's a good resolution to our anger.

> *"My God, my God, why have you forsaken me? Why are you so far from saving me, so far from my cries of anguish? My God, I cry out by day, but you do not answer, by night, but I find no rest.*
>
> *Yet you are enthroned as the Holy One; you are the one Israel praises. In you our ancestors put their trust; they trusted and you delivered them. To you they cried out and were saved; in you they trusted and were not put to shame.*
>
> *But I am a worm and not a man, scorned by everyone, despised by the people."*

Psalm 22:1-6 (NIV)

After David's whining and complaining subsided, in the same book he started praising God. Psalm 22:22-24 (NIV) reads:

> *"I will declare your name to my people; in the assembly I will praise you. You who fear the Lord, praise him! All you descendants of Jacob, honor him! Revere him, all you descendants of Israel! For he has not despised or scorned the suffering of the afflicted one; he has not hidden his face from him but has listened to his cry for help."*

## AWARE AND ATTENTIVE

I definitely feel a calling to help the Church become more informed. Be mindful that there are a lot of hurting people—Christian people—who are losing their hope and want to put an end to their despair and torment.

Christians who succumb to suicide are more common than we suspect. Since Rick's death in 2009, I know of five suicides among Christian people within my sphere. We must be aware and attentive. Someone we know and love could possibly be battling with suicidal thoughts—even going to the extreme of taking their own life. As I've said earlier, we need to realize if we talk about it openly, it strips the devil of power.

I am thankful that suicide is not the unpardonable sin. People do not enter heaven because they have done good deeds in this life. People go to heaven because they have accepted Jesus Christ as their God and Savior.

# 14

## Bitterness to Beauty

### LEMONS

As it says in the song, "Lemon tree very pretty and the lemon flower is sweet, but the fruit of the poor lemon is impossible to eat."[1] As Christians we try and live our lives as that beautiful fruit tree. In our endeavors to live a joyous life—the life that Christ intended for us to live—we get sidetracked. Through devastation, heartache, and tragedies, things can quickly turn sour, just like the fruit on the lemon tree.

Everything can be going well—savoring life, enjoying our kids, grandkids and our friends. God is using us for His glory and all is well with the world. Then, suddenly, something disastrous happens and our existence changes. This is, "where the rubber meets the road." Do we hold on to our faith or do we turn our backs on God?

At times, the road seems so hard and our faith so little. We want people to believe we are okay, when in fact we are hurting on the inside. Sometimes we can be too proud to seek out the prayer and the help we may need—thinking we can "get over it." We plaster a fake smile on our face so people will perceive us as an overcomer—a person who always "has it all together."

Just as the juice is squeezed from a lemon we may feel squeezed. The squeezing process is extremely difficult and can cause confusion and havoc in our lives. My husband felt this squeezing, but didn't reach out and receive the help he needed. Perhaps, he was too proud, and thought it would make him look weak in front of his peers.

It's at these times that we need to decide how to live our lives. When difficulties come, do we wallow in bitterness or do we persevere through the trial and come out as a sweet refreshing drink?

## LACE

Lace is a beautiful, delicate fabric. It is made with painstaking craftsmanship and its beauty is undeniable, although not as popular as it was in former days. "Early references to 'lace' in English texts almost certainly refer to 'ties', as this was the primary meaning of the word lace until well into the seventeenth century."[2]

The day I found my beautiful *dress on the tree* was a day that symbolized new life for me. I didn't know at the time I purchased the dress for a dollar that it would signify a change in my life. It was adorned with elegant lace. I can now see, as The Master Weaver cut off old soul *ties*, He began to weave fresh *ties* into my new life.

## ONE FAITHFUL GOD

I know if I hadn't had faith in the Lord I would not be where I am today. I'm enjoying the blessings of God, with a tremendous husband, great kids and wonderful grand-children. I'm living a life that many women my age would be delighted to have. Although the journey has been difficult, I'm happy to say that I still put my trust in Jesus.

My hope for this book is to encourage anyone going through dire circumstances to run towards God and not away from Him. Allow Him to weave the sour and bitter circumstances of your life into beautiful lace. This will speak of the work He has done in you and give you the opportunity to be a testimony of God's grace and mercy—just as He has done for me.

# Endnotes

1. Peter, Paul and Mary. "Lemon Tree Very Pretty." By Will Holt *If I Had a Hammer.* Warner Bros 1962. LP.

2. The Origins of Lace. Retreived from: https://www. laceguild.org/craft/history.html

# Widow's Poem

He's gone oh Lord, how can this be
The man, that you have given me.
My heart is broken, my will is crushed
The tears fall down, they can't be hushed.

A blow that strikes you on your heart
A dreaded thing, sharp as a dart.
You lose your love, the one so dear
A piece of you, it's so unclear?

I must move forward, that I know
Get through the grief and let it go
It's all so hard, you can't deny.
This loss I have… must say goodbye.

I'm thankful God that he's with you
It helps me breathe and make it through.
If I would have one thing to say
Lord help the Widows, this I pray.

*By: Pam Fleming, 2011*

# Recommended Resources

## BOOKS

1. Hess, Dave. *Hope Beyond Reason*. Createspace Independent Publishing Platform, 2014.

2. Hess, Dave. *Hope Beyond Disappointment*. Createspace Independent Publishing Platform, 2013.

3. Cline, Stacy. *Suffering Loss*. Furrow Press, 2009.

4. Gardener, Thom. *Healing the Wounded Heart*, Destiny Image Publishers, 2005.

5. Stanley, Charles. *When Tragedy Strikes,* Thomas Nelson, 2004.

6. Wright, H. Norman. *Experiencing Grief.* B&H Books, 2004.

7. Biebel, David B. (DMin) and Foster, Suzanne L. (MA), *Finding Your Way after the Suicide of Someone You Love.* Zondervan, 2005.

## INSPIRATIONAL SCRIPTURE

- 2 Corinthians 12:9 (NIV)

  *"…'My grace is sufficient for you, for my power is made perfect in weakness.' Therefore I will boast all the more gladly about my weaknesses, so that Christ's power may rest on me."*

- Matthew 2:18 (NET)

  *"A voice was heard in Ramah, weeping and loud wailing, Rachel weeping for her children; and she did not want to be comforted, because they were gone."*

- Psalm 30:11-12 (NIV)

  *"You have turned for me my mourning into dancing; You have put off my sackcloth and clothed me with gladness, to the end that my glory may sing praise to You and not be*

silent. O Lord my God, I will give thanks to You forever."

- Mark 10:9 (ESV)

  *"What therefore God has joined together, let no man separate."*

- Psalm 127:3 (NASB)

  *"Behold, children are a heritage from the Lord, offspring a reward from him."*

- Psalm 118:17 (KJV)

  *"I shall not die, but live, and declare the works of the Lord."*

- Psalm 9:1-2 (NKJV)

  *"I will praise You, O Lord, with my whole heart; I will tell of all Your marvelous works. I will be glad and rejoice in You; I will sing praise to Your name, O Most High."*

- Proverbs 4:21-22 (KJV)

  *"My son, attend to my words; incline thine ear unto my sayings. Let them not depart from thine eyes; keep them in the midst of thine heart. For they are life unto those that find them, and health to all their flesh."*

- Proverbs 17:22 (NLT)

  *"A cheerful heart is good medicine, but a broken spirit saps a person's strength."*

- Romans 8:28 (NKJV)

  *"And we know that all things work together for good to those who love God, to those who are the called according to his purpose."*

- Proverbs 27:9 (NLT)

  *"The heartfelt counsel of a friend is as sweet as perfume and incense."*

- 2 Samuel 11:1 (NASB)

  *"Then it happened in the spring, at the time when kings go out to battle, that David sent Joab and his servants with him and all Israel, and they destroyed the sons of Ammon and besieged Rabbah. But David stayed at Jerusalem."*

- Matthew 18:10 (NASB)

  *"See that you do not despise one of these little ones, for I say to you that their angels in heaven continually see the face of My Father who is in heaven."*

- Psalm 107:13-14 (NKJV)

  *"Then they cried out to the Lord in their trouble, and He saved them out of their distresses. He brought them out of darkness and their show of death, and broke their chains in pieces."*

- James 1:27 (KJV)

  *"Pure religion and undefiled before God and the Father is this, to visit the fatherless and widows in their affliction, and to keep himself unspotted from the world."*

- Psalm 107:13-14 (NKJV)

  *"Then they cried out to the LORD in their trouble, and He saved them out of their distresses. He brought them out of darkness and the shadow of death, and broke their chains in pieces."*

- Job 23: 8-10 (NIV)

  *"But if I go to the east, he is not there; if I go to the west, I do not find him. When he is at work in the north, I do not see him; when he turns to the south, I catch no glimpse of him. But he knows the way that I take; when he has tested me, I will come forth as gold."*

- Isaiah 40:11 (NIV)

  *"He tends his flock like a shepherd: He gathers the lambs in his arms and carries them close to his heart; he gently leads those that have young."*

- 2 Corinthians 10:4 (NIV)

  *"The weapons we fight with are not the weapons of the world. On the contrary, they have divine power to demolish strongholds."*

- James 1:25 (NLT)

  *"But if you look carefully into the perfect law that sets you free, and if you do what it says and don't forget what you heard, then God will bless you for doing it."*

- Isaiah 61:3 (NKJV)

  *"...to give them beauty for ashes, the oil of joy for mourning, the garment of praise for the spirit of heaviness..."*

- Isaiah 58:6 (NLT)

  *"No, this is the kind of fasting I want: Free those who are wrongly imprisoned; lighten*

*the burden of those who work for you. Let the oppressed go free, and remove the chains that bind people."*

- 1 Thessalonians 5:11 (NIV)

  *"Therefore encourage one another and build each other up, just as in fact you are doing."*

- James 5:16 (NIV)

  *"Therefore confess your sins to each other and pray for each other so that you may be healed. The prayer of a righteous person is powerful and effective."*

- Isaiah 54:5 (KJV)

  *"For thy Maker is thine husband; the LORD of hosts is his name..."*

- Psalm 68:5 (ESV)

  *"Father of the fatherless and protector of widows is God in his holy habitation"*

- Ecclesiastes 4:9-10 (NASB)

  *"Two are better than one because they have a good return for their labor. For if either of*

*them falls, the one will lift up his companion. But woe to the one who falls when there is not another to lift him up."*

- Psalm 34: 17-18 (NIV)

  *"The righteous cry out, and the LORD hears them; He delivers them from all their troubles. The LORD is close to the brokenhearted and saves those who are crushed in spirit"*

- Isaiah 61:7 (NKJV)

  *"Instead of your shame you shall have a double honor, and instead of confusion they shall rejoice in their portion. Therefore in their land they shall possess double, everlasting joy shall be theirs."*

- 1 Samuel 16:7 (ESV)

  *"…man looks on the outward appearance, but the LORD looks on the heart."*

- Luke 21:26 (NASB)

  *"Men fainting from fear and the expectation of the things which are coming upon the world; for the powers of the heavens will be shaken."*

- Psalm 91:4-6 (NIV)

  *"He will cover you with his feathers, and under his wings you will find refuge; his faithfulness will be your shield and rampart. You will not fear the terror of night, nor the arrow that flies by day, nor the pestilence that stalks in the darkness, nor the plague that destroys at midday."*

- Proverbs 17:22 (AMP)

  *"A happy heart is good medicine and a cheerful mind works healing, but a broken spirit dries up the bones."*

- Isaiah 61:3 (NIV)

  *"And provide for those who grieve in Zion— to bestow on them a crown of beauty instead of ashes, the oil of joy instead of mourning, and a garment of praise instead of a spirit of despair...."*

- I Samuel 15:22 (NIV)

  *"...Does the LORD delight in burnt offerings and sacrifices as much as in obeying the LORD? To obey is better than sacrifice,..."*

- Hebrews 10:26 (NIV)

  *"If we deliberately keep on sinning after we have received the knowledge of the truth, no sacrifice for sins is left."*

- Psalm 22:1-2 (NIV)

  *"My God, my God, why have you forsaken me? Why are you so far from saving me, so far from my cries of anguish? My God, I cry out by day, but you do not answer, by night, but I find no rest."*

- Psalm 22:3-5 (NIV)

  *"Yet you are enthroned as the Holy One; you are the one Israel praises. In you our ancestors put their trust; they trusted and you delivered them. To you they cried out and were saved; in you they trusted and were not put to shame."*

- Psalm 22:6 (NIV)

  *"But I am a worm and not a man, scorned by everyone, despised by the people."*

- Psalm 22:22-24 (NIV)

  *"I will declare your name to my people; in the assembly I will praise you. You who fear the*

*Lord, praise him! All you descendants of Jacob, honor him! Revere him, all you descendants of Israel! For he has not despised or scorned the suffering of the afflicted one; he has not hidden his face from him but has listened to his cry for help."*

- Ephesians 2:8 (NIV)

  *"For it is by grace you have been saved, through faith—and this is not from your-selves, it is the gift of God."*

# Other Healing Resources

**Church Attendance**—even if you don't feel like it. Feed your spirit.

**A Counselor**—someone you trust - to meet with, pray with, confide in, and hold you accountable.

**Support Groups**—I tried several of these and while some didn't work, other types of counseling did. Be sure to reach out and get help. You are worth it.

**Life Coaches**—So beneficial in getting your life back on track.

**Friends**—Are priceless. If you don't have any—pray and ask the Lord to bring them. Be proactive and reach out to people and pastors in your church or other Christians in your community. You need to have connection to others.

***Physical Care***—Get your nails done, get your hair done. Eating right, massages, regular physical exams, exercise, and vitamins are some of my recommendations for taking care of your body. Sudden adversities are very stressful on our temples. Remember the Lord lives in you and to take care of His house the best you can.